# CONTENTS

# The author

David Ventura read music at Edinburgh University, has taught music in Scotland, Lanca-shire, Liverpool and the Isle of Wight and was the director of music at Hereford Sixth Form College for fifteen years up until 2009. He has lectured nationwide on music tech-nology and advised the UK Government on assessment in the National Curriculum for music at all key stages. He has acted as a consultant for the Qualifications and Curric-ulum Authority, was chair of the Southern Examining Group's GCSE panel, examined for a number of boards, and has also run many teacher-training courses for Keynote Education. He is a prolific composer and enjoys playing jazz piano.

# Acknowledgements

David Ventura would like to thank Mat Walters and Anthony Osborne, who provided invaluable advice and resources, for their support and assistance during the preparation of this book.

The author would also like to thank Mark Wilderspin for his advice and suggestions as well as Lucien Jenkins, Chris Elcombe, Rose Vickridge, Sam Queen and Katherine Smith of Rhinegold Publishing for their assistance throughout the editing and produc-tion process. Also Claudine Nightingale for her invaluable help in preparing the second edition.

# Film Music

## IN FOCUS
### David Ventura

# SECOND EDITION

R·

Rhinegold Education
239–241 Shaftesbury Avenue
London WC2H 8TF

## Music Study Guides

GCSE, AS and A2 Music Study Guides (AQA, Edexcel and OCR)
GCSE, AS and A2 Music Listening Tests (AQA, Edexcel and OCR)
AS/A2 Music Technology Study Guide (Edexcel)
AS/A2 Music Technology Listening Tests (Edexcel)
Revision Guides for GCSE (AQA, Edexcel and OCR), AS and A2 Music (Edexcel)

## Other Rhinegold Study Guides

Rhinegold publishes resources for candidates studying Drama and Theatre Studies

## Also available from Rhinegold Education

Key Stage 3 Listening Tests: Book 1 and Book 2
AS and A2 Music Harmony Workbooks
GCSE and AS Music Composition Workbooks
GCSE and AS Music Literacy Workbooks
Romanticism in Focus, Baroque Music in Focus, Film Music in Focus, Modernism in Focus,
*The Immaculate Collection in Focus*, *Who's Next* in Focus, *Batman* in Focus,
*Goldfinger* in Focus, Musicals in Focus, Music Technology from Scratch,
You Can Teach Primary Music

Rhinegold also publishes Choir & Organ, Classical Music, Classroom Music,
Early Music Today, International Piano, Music Teacher, Muso, Opera Now, Piano, The Singer,
Teaching Drama, British and International Music Yearbook, British Performing Arts Yearbook,
British Music Education Yearbook, World Conservatoires,
Rhinegold Dictionary of Music in Sound

First published 2008 in Great Britain by
Rhinegold Education
239–241 Shaftesbury Avenue
London WC2H 8TF

Telephone: 020 7333 1720
Fax: 020 7333 1765

www.rhinegold.co.uk

## Film Music in Focus (2nd edition)

British Library Cataloguing in Publication Data.
*A catalogue record for this book is available from the British Library.*

ISBN: 978-1-907447-08-2

Printed and bound by Information Press Ltd, Eynsham, Oxford

# 1. BACKGROUND INFORMATION

The purpose of this book is to provide a general introduction to music for film. The first two chapters contain some background information about the history of film music, its context and influences, and an explanation of some of the main technical practices and procedures of the industry. The main part of the book is devoted to outlining the common film genres, with representative composers from each and an analysis of one or two of their well-known film scores. In order to keep the text relatively succinct it has been necessary to leave out many scores that film buffs would consider seminal. In addition it should be remembered that many composers employ an extended range of styles in their scores. To bind them to a specific genre is clearly an oversimplification.

This book has in part been written to meet the needs of music students and therefore the scores are frequently explained using technical language. It is hoped the glossary will help those who are less familiar with the musical terms used. I have also borne in mind the needs of students working in film studies in sixth form colleges and FE, and the requirements of the Creative and Media Diploma. How it will be useful for these examinations is explained in a new chapter (p. 94). Finally, I hope it to be of value and interest to anyone wishing to enhance their experience of going to the movies.

## Cinema in context

Bustling crowds in the Roxy Theatre, New York

Film-making is a relatively new art form. It is not surprising, therefore, that its development has not been particularly smooth. In the United States, in 1927, the Roxy Theater (dubbed 'The Cathedral of

See *Film Music – A Neglected Art* by Roy M Prendergast (WW Norton and Company 1992).

the Motion Picture') opened in New York, with a 6,200-seat capacity. In 1938, 65% of the American public went to the movies every week. Yet by the early 1960s the film industry was in decline, while television was in the ascendancy. Cinemas were closing down or being converted into bingo palaces. In the past 20 years, however, the film industry has undergone a remarkable recovery, with regular productions of Hollywood blockbusters and online DVD rental reinvigorating the market.

Like theatre before it, film has had a powerful influence on public opinion and, in turn, political thinking, in partnership with the more immediate medium of television. Examples of influential films include *The Full Monty* (1997), a black comedy that explores the effects of unemployment in the north of England, and *Jarhead* (2005), with its realistic portrayal of the Gulf War. The Hollywood media circus finds its way into all walks of life, being reported in the press, magazines and television, and shaping the views of many of the public, both young and old. The triumph of good over evil is a subject that can be found in novels and plays throughout the history of communication. Modern film provides a vehicle for this and other universal themes, portraying them both graphically and entertainingly.

This is not to say that films cannot convey a subtle or subliminal message. *In the Heat of the Night* (1967) carries a powerful message concerning the racism found in a small town, but also includes the subtext of a lonely, boozy and bigoted policeman. *The Deer Hunter* (1978) and *The Pianist* (2002) examine how war destroys individual lives, rather than celebrating the exploits of a daring hero.

If one assumes that cinema audiences generally do not go out for an evening's education or moral lecture, it may seem remarkable to consider the number of films that carry an important social message. On the other hand, film is the medium through which these messages can reach the widest audiences. In the modern world, a work of art or even a novel doesn't have the same scope for influencing opinion. Film makers know this and exploit it.

Music helps a film communicate its ideas. A film about an alcoholic (*The Lost Weekend*, 1945) was released without any music and had to be withdrawn from

See *Complete Guide to Film Scoring* by Richard Davis (Berklee Press 1999).

cinemas because the audience giggled at the most dramatic moments. A music score, composed by Miklós Rózsa, was added to the film at a later date and the film was re-released to critical acclaim (even though Rózsa remained unacknowledged). André Previn has demonstrated to television audiences how a gruesome murder scene in a kitchen is reduced to farce when the soundtrack is muted.

The following pages will present some of the techniques composers use to write film music and the problems they encounter along the way, together with an explanation of some of the terminology used by the film industry.

# The purpose of music in film

From the very early days of silent movies, music was considered essential to the moving image. At this point, its prime purpose was to disguise the noise of the

> *The Jazz Singer* (1927) was the first commercially successful sound film.

projectors and prevent the audience from feeling a sense of disembodiment, caused by the rather surreal, ghost-like quality of the images projected onto the screen. With the arrival of 'talkies', there was a brief period when music was thought to distract an audience from following the dialogue in a film (with the obvious exception of musicals). However, it soon returned to take a central place in film-making: for the most part, music is essential to story-telling and without it, the audience's engagement with the narrative is considerably reduced.

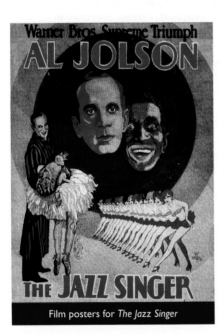

Film posters for *The Jazz Singer*

Music can be used in a variety of ways in a film, depending on the film's aims and the techniques employed by the director. The more obvious uses are listed below:

- To create or enhance a mood
- To function as a leitmotif, linked to the appearance of a character or idea or to remind us of one not actually present on screen
- To link one scene to another or smooth over visual cuts, providing continuity
- To emphasise a gesture (this is known as 'mickey-mousing')
- To give additional commercial impetus
- To provide unexpected juxtapositions – for instance, Pippin's sad unaccompanied song that goes with the attack by the forces of Gondor on Osgiliath in *Lord of the Rings: Return of the King* (2003) or to provide irony – for instance, the torture scene in *Reservoir Dogs* (1992) is accompanied by Stealer's Wheel's *Stuck in the Middle with You*
- To illustrate geographic location and historical period
- To influence the pacing of a scene (making it appear faster/slower/more comprehensive) – for instance in action sequences.

# How film scores are produced

The initial idea for a film may come from a number of sources. It might be adapted from a successful book or stage play, or simply from a well-known story, fictional or otherwise. It may be conceived by the writer or director, or be an idea held dear by a rich entrepreneur. Whatever the source, once the initial concept for a film has been established, a screenplay needs to be written and a producer and director engaged.

When it comes to making the film, there are a huge number of people involved. Below is a list of the key personnel, including the sound crew:

- **Writer**: converts the story or stage play into a screenplay (script).
- **Producer**: responsible for the financial arrangements and overall organisation of the film, hiring the actors and the rest of the many people involved. Keeps a close eye on the schedule and is responsible to the studio executives.
- **Director**: looks after the creative side, approves the script, oversees the overall look of the film, including lighting, costumes, set and so on, and directs the actors during filming. Supervises the editing of the film after shooting.
- **Composer**: writes the musical score and helps with its recording. May conduct a studio orchestra.
- **Orchestrator**: in most films the composer is given very little time to write the music and usually doesn't have time to orchestrate it as well. The composer will produce either a short score or a MIDI recording and then pass it on to a team of orchestrators.
- **Copyist**: writes out, or uses music software to produce, the individual instrumental or vocal parts from the orchestrator's full score.
- **Music editor**: responsible for technical aspects such as synchronisation of recorded music to the visuals – consequently, will be familiar with the latest music software. Works closely with the composer and produces a master cue list and timing notes. Sometimes makes amendments to the score at the request of the director. A film editor may sometimes cut scenes to music to achieve a sense of flow or pace and the music editor assists in this.

In recent times the roles of the music editor and music supervisor have become blurred. Jobs such as supervising sound editor can take on creative and organisational functions post-production.

- **Music supervisor**: takes care of any music that needs to be imported, such as source music or non-diegetic music that has not been especially composed. If songs are being used then they negotiate rights and organise any re-recording needed.
- **Foley editor**: responsible for sound effects recorded from natural sounds.
- **Mixer/recordist**: on-set responsibility for recording dialogue.
- **Sound designer**: responsible for the overall sound of the film. Works with the producer and director at the start, and may take on some work post-production, particularly if synthesisers and electronic sound are involved.

■ **Re-recording mixer/dubbing mixer**: combines the music, dialogue and sound effects to produce the final soundtrack; works in a team with engineers, composer, director and producer.

There are also a number of technical terms that are used in films, as well as some musical vocabulary used in this book, that need some explanation – see the glossary chapter at the end of the book.

# The composer's experience

Although an established composer may be brought in for discussions at an early stage in the film-making process, most of the music is composed once filming is complete. The composer is sent a 'locked' version of the film and shortly afterwards attends a spotting session to view it with the producer, director, music editor and sound designer. A spotting session is when decisions are made as to where music is needed in the film. The various music cues are noted down by the music editor to help the composer with timing.

There are a few instances in film history where parts of the underscore have been taken into account during filming, notably Prokofiev's music for Eisenstein's *Alexander Nevsky* (1938) and Bernard Herrmann's score for Orson Welles' *Citizen Kane* (1941) (note that only some of this score was pre-recorded).

The composer then only has a few weeks to complete and record the score. As this process progresses music cues are sent to the director, sometimes in electronic format – such as MP3 – which give an idea of the composer's mix. When they are approved they are sent onwards, often as MIDI files, to orchestrators and copyists. The score is then recorded and the music editor has to ensure synchronisation between sound and picture.

Before digital technology made this job more controllable, an editor would have had to rely on streamers and punches. This is where the film is scratched, progressively moving across the frames (streamers) until a hit point is reached and the frame is pushed through (punches). The orchestra conductor will then see a white line moving across the projected image and a flash for the hit point. With digital technology music recordings can be 'time stretched' by small amounts without a noticeable reduction in quality and made to fit the moving image very accurately.

When the music recording has been approved it is then mixed and dubbed with sound effects and dialogue. The entire process is very pressurised and composers have to learn to cope with this. With the demise of the big studios in the 1950s the music production team wasn't always available, but this coincided with smaller ensembles and scores, and pop music tracks. Modern blockbusters have restored the orchestra to a dominant position within the film, and once again teams of musicians have to work together to produce a final product.

# 2. INFLUENCES: A SHORT HISTORY OF CINEMA SOUND

## Music and narrative through history

The ancient Greeks can loosely be credited with the invention of opera, combining a scripted and normally narrative stage play with music in such a way that the story was enhanced by the combination of art forms. Dance and music were, from their earliest beginnings, interdependent. The need to escape from the daily routine, to exorcise the ghosts of the unknown and unexplained environment, is manifested in early cave paintings and religious rituals.

As Western-European society developed its own complex culture, dance and theatre became more formalised. In medieval times the touring mummers' plays would entertain ordinary people in street presentations with humorous re-enactments of well-known Bible stories, sometimes accompanied by pipes, drums and stringed instruments. In the Renaissance, as the population gained confidence in the ability of the individual to control their own destiny, music developed into an art form designed to communicate important messages, whether sacred or profane. At the start of the 17th century a new form of opera came into existence, based on what the early-Florentine *camerata* believed to be ancient Greek practice. The genre soon left the patronage of the ducal courts and public opera houses sprang up throughout Italy. The growing and moneyed middle classes quickly spotted investment opportunities in this new craze and theatres were equipped with all manner of technical devices to make productions more exciting, developing particularly the illusion of the supernatural or divine.

> The Florentine camerata was a group of poets and musicians who met at the houses of aristocrats in the late 16th century. Their discussions were instrumental in the development of early opera.

The operas of Mozart (1756–1791) broke away from the standard line of classical themes, incorporating real-life drama and situation comedies. Weber (1786–1826) exploited the public taste for supernatural magic and by the mid-19th century, opera had developed to such an extent that Wagner (1813–1883) had to have a special theatre built for him in Bayreuth to realise the ambitious projects he had in mind. Along with his extensive production values, Wagner's approach to opera blurred the distinctions between the different forms of musical communication – that is, aria or song for the emotional peaks of the plot and recitative for the faster-moving speech and dramatic action sequences – to create a new type of music-drama. Through the use of these techniques the music took on a new, less subservient role, functioning at a different level by supplying a psychological commentary on the plot. The large orchestra Wagner employed could be given the role of supplying leitmotifs to represent a person, object or idea/concept, thus strengthening the delivery of the story line and helping to communicate its often complex sub-plots and subliminal messages.

Operas and operettas did not constitute the only use of music in the theatre, however. Stage plays frequently deployed incidental music to aid the creation of atmosphere and set the scene. Mendelssohn (1809–1847) wrote music for Shakespeare's *A Midsummer Night's Dream* (1842) which perfectly captures the gossamer lightness of the fairies, in contrast to the clumsiness of Bottom as a donkey. In ballet too, music was there not just for dancing to, but also to help create the illusion of time and place.

Composers of the 17th–19th centuries, then, were familiar with providing music to enhance stage action. They were, of course, also skilled in writing music for imaginary scenes or illustrations of story lines. Programme music has a long tradition. The Elizabethan composer John Bull (c.1562–1628) wrote 'battle music' for the virginal (an English table harpsichord) and Vivaldi's (1678–1741) four violin concertos depicting the four seasons are now perhaps the most famous of all Baroque instrumental compositions. Beethoven's (1770–1827) Symphony No 6 in F (written 1807–1808), with its pastoral descriptive scenes, was the precursor to a blossoming of programme music composition in the 19th century. This period of Romantic music included the symphonic poems of Liszt and the delicate scene-painting of Sibelius's *Swan of Tuonela* (1893) and Debussy's *Prélude à l'Après-midi d'un faune* (1894).

# Music and film: the early days

Projecting moving images to a paying audience began in 1895 in Paris with a series of short scenes from everyday life by the Lumière brothers. This followed on from the pioneering work of the American inventor Thomas Edison, who in 1891 built a kinetoscope. As the 20th century progressed the film industry steadily grew until, in the 1920s, Hollywood was producing on average 800 films per year.

The kinetoscope was not a movie projector as we understand them today – it was designed for films to be viewed by individuals, through the window of a cabinet – but it introduced the basic approach that would become the standard for all subsequent cinematic projection.

Throughout this decade films became increasingly polished and also grew in length. Even in these early days of film production, clear genres could be identified. Top of the list was the swashbuckling adventure movie, but there were also many biblical epics, westerns, romances, mysteries, horrors, melodramas and comedies. During this period production, distribution and exhibition of the films became controlled under one roof, by five major production companies: MGM, Fox (later to become 20th Century Fox), Paramount Pictures, RKO and Warner Brothers.

# Influences: a short history of cinema sound

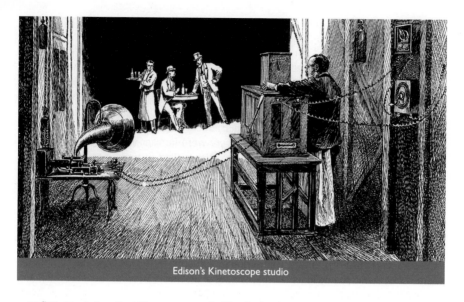

Edison's Kinetoscope studio

At first, music for silent films was supplied live in the theatres, and for reasons other than artistic value (as mentioned in the previous chapter). Gradually, however, film production companies began to supply suggestions for music to use for particular scenes and theatre musicians would improvise music to fit. In 1912, Max Winkler began writing cue sheets – selections of music to correspond with particular kinds of scenes. Giuseppe Becce's 'Kino-bibliothek' (1919) supplied many pieces of descriptive music organised by style and mood. A huge volume entitled *Motion Picture Moods for Pianists and Organists* (1924) supplied many titles from the classical repertoire which quickly became stereotypical of particular genres.

Small theatres employed a pianist or organist, who drew upon the available libraries of music to piece together a partly improvised soundtrack, the latter utilising specially invented cinema organs that featured a large range of percussion and mechanical sound effects. Larger establishments, however, were able to afford an ensemble of musicians or even an orchestra. Rather than drawing upon improvisatory techniques they used written scores and cue sheets. A music director (or, as they were then called, a 'music illustrator') watched the film in advance and chose appropriate music for the orchestra to play during the screening. Usually this was taken from stock repertoire, but occasionally it was chosen from the work of one particular composer, giving the film an unprecedented level of musical unity.

A number of famous composers wrote scores for films during the silent era – most notably, Honegger (1892–1955), Milhaud (1892–1974) and Shostakovich (1906–1975). However, they remained exceptions to the rule.

Conductors also sometimes wrote supplementary material themselves to help ease transitions between scenes. However, at this stage in the history of film, it was difficult to synchronise the music with the visuals, despite Edison's earlier experiments and a number of technological inventions to help.

# The advent of 'talkies'

It wasn't until the release of *The Jazz Singer* (1927) that the era of silent films began its steady decline. There had been a successful attempt at a synchronised music track produced by Warner Brothers a year earlier (*Don Juan,* 1926), but it was *The Jazz Singer*, in which Al Jolson sings six songs with several sections of synchronised speech, that convinced the industry that money could be made from the 'talkies'. Sound films began to dominate throughout the 1930s: the orchestra pits were soon empty and the libraries of sheet music consigned to the bin.

> When sound films became the norm, the electric 'Wurlitzer' organ took the place of the orchestra, producing entertainment music for the interval.

Musicians involved in the industry were concerned about this new development. Following the success of *The Jazz Singer*, studios initially produced large quantities of musicals, but the public soon grew tired of these and dramatic films were produced instead, which concentrated primarily on dialogue. As a result many musicians found themselves out of work. Furthermore, the cameras were so noisy they were often enclosed in soundproofed rooms. Consequently cameramen were unable to move around freely, so films often looking visually stilted.

It wasn't long, though, before directors realised that music was essential in a film, to enhance a love scene or stir up patriotic feeling in an audience during a battle sequence. However, there remained significant technical problems to overcome. The longer films demanded a team of composers, which could often result in a disunity of style. Sound recording was primitive and some instruments, especially violins, lost their lower partials on playback, resulting in a weak sound. Some composers even resorted to reducing the numbers of strings (for instance, Arthur Benjamin in *The Man Who Knew Too Much*, 1956). The biggest problem, however, was that sound technology hadn't yet sufficiently developed to allow music to be recorded after the filming had taken place, and therefore musicians had to be present in the studio most of the time, making the whole affair very expensive. In any case, where was the realism in music being played during a love scene? It was sometimes the case that a wandering gypsy violinist would have to appear in shot to provide emotional music to fit such a scene (as mentioned by Max Steiner, quoted in *Film Music – A Neglected Art* by Roy M Prendergast (W W Norton and Company 1977)). To have specially written music would add to the cost, particularly if it was scored for full orchestra.

Around 1931 the technology to re-record a soundtrack away from the main 'sound stage' or film set became available. Now, the music, dialogue and sound effects could all be mixed in a process known as dubbing, which made the task of providing sound for a film more flexible and less expensive. The scene was set for the Golden Age of the Hollywood movies, from the late 1930s though to the 1950s.

13

# The Golden Age

This period became known as the Golden Age because of the large numbers of films that were released at the time to satisfy the demands of an American cinema audience that, in 1938, represented 65% of the population. The powerful studios that had grown up in the silent film era readily adapted to the commercial pressures and in terms of film sound, they soon established music departments which were organised along factory production lines.

From the 1920s through to the 1940s there was an influx of skilled composers and musicians from Eastern Europe – many of Jewish descent, artistic refugees from two world wars – arriving in America. They brought with them the musical skills needed for this expanding industry: compositional techniques related to theatrical productions such as the use of leitmotifs and motivic development, an understanding of writing for large orchestras, and a harmonic and melodic style that could enhance the roller-coaster of emotional expression needed to match the popular story lines of the time.

The late-Romantic style of composers such as Wagner, Brahms, Richard Strauss and Mahler was to prove ideal for Hollywood films. In the early years of the 1920s, musical scores often played almost continuously throughout films. With so much music required, studios frequently employed whole teams of composers, orchestrators and copyists.

The leading composers who used this Post-Romantic style include Max Steiner, Erich Korngold, Miklós Rózsa and Franz Waxman, all European émigrés.

As the 1940s progressed, composers began to write music that employed a more contemporary musical language. The leading American classical composer at the time was Aaron Copland (1900–1990), who developed a style that incorporated pentatonic folk influences and tonal harmonies with some of the more ground-breaking techniques – such as polychords, polyrhythms and tone rows – developed by Stravinsky (1882–1971), Bartók (1881–1945) and Schoenberg (1874–1951). Although Copland did write some music for films, his contribution lay more in the influence he had on others, particularly in music for westerns where his musical language was suggestive of vast American landscapes. He has a parallel in the English composer Ralph Vaughan Williams (1872–1958), who also used a folk-music-influenced modal language to accompany panoramic scenery in his music in *Scott of the Antarctic* (1948).

The acerbic styles of Bartók and Stravinsky were also direct influences on other film composers as the 1940s progressed into the 1950s. Leonard Bernstein's score for *On the Waterfront* (1954; see page 69) and Leonard Rosenman's for *East of Eden* (1955) both use a chromatic musical language with bitonal sections and aggressive rhythms to achieve their intended effect. Both films' narratives could be classed as social drama, a genre where a progressive musical style was more readily adopted by composers.

One composer stands out in particular during this period for his use of non-Romantic harmonies: as early as 1941, Bernard Herrmann, in Orson Welles's film *Citizen Kane* (1941), produced an innovative score to match this revolutionary production.

# Subsequent developments

By the beginning of the 1950s the big studios that had dominated Hollywood film production from the days of the early silent films were worried. MGM, Paramount, Universal, Columbia and 20th Century Fox had enjoyed a monopoly in the 1940s over the distribution of their films (they all owned their own theatres), but federal court action changed this. At the same time, the attractions of television were keeping the movie-going public at home. Studios initially reacted to this threat with gimmicks, such as wide-screen and 3D film, to offer something unique to entice audiences to the cinema, but this was short-lived. Instead, studios began to increase the production values of their films. Big productions such as *The Ten Commandments* (1956 – see page 29) and *Ben-Hur* (1959) were produced with the knowledge that television couldn't compete on the same scale. Television production budgets tended to be more modest than those for film and sometimes this could compromise artistic values. The film industry survived, but only after some radical changes.

As far as film music was concerned, there was a growth in music written for smaller instrumental ensembles, rather than the large symphony orchestra. Jazz idioms had been used in the Tennessee Williams drama, *A Streetcar Named Desire* (1951), but much of this was source (or diegetic) music and an orchestra was also used for the credits and some tense cues. In Elmer Bernstein's score for *The Man with the Golden Arm* (1955) we hear a deliberately powerful big-band jazz sound, perhaps to complement the drug-related plot. This isn't a genuine jazz score however. Jazz requires improvisation, and apart from drummer Shelley Mann's contribution, Bernstein produced a notated score (the lead character played by Frank Sinatra was a drummer in a band, so there is a substantial use of diegetic music). Improvisation does not fit well with the prescribed timings of the screen. Away from the home of jazz, in France, the director and writer Louis Malle had gathered together a group of musicians, including Miles Davis, to record a soundtrack for his film *Ascenseur pour l'échafaud* (1958), which introduced improvisation as an important element. There have, of course, been a number of movies that feature jazz as diegetic music, such as musicals or biographies. A notable semi-fictional example is Clint Eastwood's biography of saxophonist Charlie Parker, *Bird* (1988).

A similar case of written music with improvised solos can be found in the score for the Duke Ellington orchestra penned by Billy Strayhorn and used in the film *Anatomy of a Murder* (1959).

Popular music was introduced gradually into soundtracks in the 1950s. The success of David Raksin's score for *Laura* (1944 – see page 37) showed film studios that a tune that could be played, danced to or arranged for different instrumental ensembles, with the possible addition of lyrics, providing an extra marketing tool beyond the film's box-office revenue. Raksin's chromatic, jazz-ballad theme permeates the movie as its single musical motif and its haunting quality remains in the listener's memory long after the film has finished. Henry Mancini's score for *Breakfast at Tiffany's* (1961) has a similarly powerful effect. The melody of *Moon River* has reappeared countless times in dance band and orchestral arrangements. It is interesting to note, however, that Mancini uses this memorable tune economically in the film itself, in places only hinting at its melodic outline, leaving the audience wanting more.

In *Blackboard Jungle* (1955), jazz music is used to signify the establishment. Teenage aggression is represented by Bill Hailey and the Comets' *Rock Around the Clock* under the film's opening credits. This record gained huge sales after the film was released and the music contrasts well with the more staid jazz tracks played by the classroom teacher. Pop and rock music idioms were not used by composers of film scores which needed to be tied closely to the narrative: the particular structure of a pop soundtrack is not sufficiently adaptable to be used as underscore and much rock music is likely to be obtrusive. However, from the 1960s studios imported pop tracks into films, creating the possibility of music sales on top of the box office receipts.

A notable early example of this can be found in *The Graduate* (1967), which includes a number of pop hit tracks by Simon and Garfunkel. This music added a new dimension to the narrative, creating an atmosphere that complemented some of the dreamlike sequences. The use of multiple inserts of soundtracks can be traced to *Easy Rider* (1969) which uses rock music tracks to enhance the biking sequences across America and is common practice today in films such as *Trainspotting* (1996) and *American Beauty* (1999). Furthermore, the musical style of the imported tracks can be used to target specific sectors of the market: the guitar-based rock of *American Pie* (1999) or the slick urban 'rare groove remix' of David Holmes's music in films such as *Ocean's Eleven* (2001) are examples of this.

The James Bond series of films is a good case in point; artists as diverse as Shirley Bassey and Paul McCartney have had success with their songs, complementing the highly successful main scores. 11 of the 14 tracks were produced by John Barry. Barry's own style is instantly recognisable, mixing brassy jazz sounds with soaring melodies, and is epitomised by the soundtrack for *Goldfinger* (1964).

Sometimes, film producers insert a single track into the film, normally to run under the closing credits, which audiences will remember when they leave the theatre. Sometimes the commercial considerations are so great that a track can be inserted during the film for the sake of it. The use of the soft rock track 'Everything I Do, I Do It For You', sung by Bryan Adams in *Robin Hood: Prince of Thieves* (1991) is an example of this as the majority of the film utilises Michael Kamen's traditional orchestral score (see page 56). The soundtracks for films such as *A Hard Day's Night* (1964) and *Titanic* (1997) have grossed more profit than the individual films themselves.

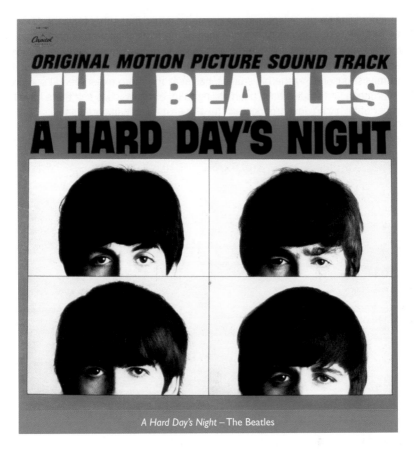

*A Hard Day's Night* – The Beatles

Despite the advent of modern music technology, comparatively few films have used electronic soundtracks. The Greek composer Vangelis had a chart success with the main theme from *Chariots of Fire* (1981), which was produced completely on analogue synthesisers. Of higher artistic merit is his score for the cult sci-fi film *Blade Runner* (1982) in which he marshals the forces of his well-equipped London studio to produce a multi-layered and atmospheric soundtrack that perfectly complements the futuristic industrial landscape of the film (see page 65). It is worth noting, however, that when a love element creeps into the narrative he resorts to piano and saxophone, albeit heavily processed. A greater number of films used electronic soundtracks as the 1980s progressed. These included Brad Fiedel's soundtracks for *The Terminator* and *Terminator 2* and the music of Wendy Carlos (famous for the seminal synthesiser album *Switched-On Bach*, released in 1968) that was used in the music for *Tron* (1982).

Recent years have seen a return to the production values of the big studios of the 1940s and along with this a return to the symphonic score in the style of Steiner and Korngold. All this is clearly

In India the Bollywood industry never really deserted the big productions. (see page 91)

very encouraging for musicians and has created a public that either buys the CD sound-tracks, or invests in video or DVD recordings of the films. Digital broadcasting and the internet are also proving viable alternatives to going to the cinema and the studios are still able to make profits this way. Meanwhile, the growth of independent productions, sometimes sponsored by the big studios, has kept the more experimental composers busy. European film studios have been willing to try out new ideas and there have been a number of highly original producers in the Far East – Japan in particular.

# 3. EARLY SOUND FILMS

## Max Steiner (1888–1971)

Max Steiner came to New York in December 1914, shortly after the outbreak of World War I. He was from a highly musical Jewish family in Vienna and received considerable early training as a musician, playing a number of orchestral instruments including the violin and trumpet as well as the piano and organ. His family circle included his godfather Richard Strauss and for a time he received piano lessons from Johannes Brahms and, while a student at the Imperial Academy of Music, Gustav Mahler. On arrival in New York he spent time on Broadway working as an orchestrator and conductor with Jerome Kern and George Gershwin before moving to Hollywood in 1929 for a job with RKO, later working extensively with Warner Brothers.

Steiner brought with him his skills as a composer in the Viennese tradition. He had a logical and direct approach to thematic development with a taste for using the leitmotif techniques of Richard Wagner and a harmonic language firmly rooted in tonality; yet he was also willing to experiment with chromatic chord progressions when needed. Steiner would have been familiar with the tone poems and operas of his godfather, Richard Strauss – works that conveyed extremes of emotion through chromatic dissonances and large orchestral forces.

Bringing the skills of a musical director to Hollywood, he worked for 35 years as a composer, creating many important film scores, including *Gone with the Wind* (1939), *Casablanca* (1942), *The Glass Menagerie* (1950) and *A Summer Place* (1959). But it was his score for *King Kong* (1933) – one of the first American films to feature an extensive musical score – that was to prove his greatest contribution to the history of music for the movies.

### King Kong (1933)

How does a composer decide which points of a film to score and which to leave silent? In silent movies the improvising pianist often provided continuous music throughout the entire film. In the early days of Hollywood there was also a large amount of music used in films (indeed, certain composers and studios favoured wall-to-wall music), but Max Steiner recognised the power of silence. There are a number of moments in *King Kong*, for instance, when the big orchestral sound is abruptly cut and replaced by sound effects: Kong's fight with a tyrannosaurus rex is one example, as is the aeroplane attack on Kong at the top of the Empire State Building. Perhaps the most telling example of restraint, however, is that following the grandiose music that accompanies the opening credits, there is no further music for a full 18 minutes, until the ship carrying the expeditionaries approaches Skull Island in the fog. For this cue a mysterious ostinato figure on the harp is used that delineates sustained string chords based on added sixths and diminished sevenths. The pattern gradually rises in anticipation, as the explorers approach Kong's domain.

The heroine is tied up to await the appearance of Kong. Steiner's music here enhances the drama with rushing chromatic sequences on the strings together with heavy brass and crashing percussion

Steiner blurs the distinction between diegetic and non-diegetic music by introducing the sound of drums as the ship nears the shore. Are these part of the non-diegetic orchestra or a sound from the island? Although they are later established as diegetic (drums are visually present in shots of the natives) there are a number of times during the film when they play in time with the background music – music that only the cinema audience can discern. This ambiguity can be disconcerting. The use of the rhythmic drum sounds permeates the whole of this section of the film. Drums interfere with the love scene on deck between Ann Darrow and John Driscoll and fade out as the romance intensifies, supplanted by more expressive and diatonically composed string music. Drums alone are used immediately after Ann's abduction by the natives and during the panic which arises when her absence is discovered by the ship's crew (they are muted during the scenes below deck to add a sense of space). Rhythm helps to build up the tension, culminating in the powerful orchestral tutti when the native ritual scene hits the screen.

Steiner's use of leitmotifs is both direct and subtle. The falling three notes played powerfully in the opening credits (C, B♮ and B♭) on the lower brass are associated with King Kong and his jungle domain. The motif associated with the heroine (Ann Darrow, played by Fay Wray) is linked to this by virtue of the common use of falling chromatic steps. This reinforces the bond that exists between the two characters – at least from Kong's point of view. There are numerous chromatic passages throughout the action, giving the overall sound a stylistic unity. The full orchestral tutti when Ann is tied up by the natives is one example: it features rising chromatic sequences and a diminution of the four-note stepped motif to increase excitement, building to a climax and then silence. Another can be heard when a slithering chromatic scale is employed to enhance the movement of the water serpent in Kong's cave.

The composer is fond of the dramatic impact of the tritone which runs through the score and he frequently employs rhythmic devices for emphasis. As with many film composers, he owed a debt to the primeval yet sophisticated musical language of Stravinsky's *Rite of Spring* (1913), but avoided the obvious convenience of mimicking it: Steiner was very much his own man.

# Erich Wolfgang Korngold (1897–1957)

Erich Wolfgang Korngold

Another Jewish émigré from Eastern Europe, Korngold was the son of a music critic and, like Steiner, counted Strauss and Mahler among his acquaintances. He achieved success in Europe as a composer of operas before moving to the United States in 1934, where he continued to compose concert music throughout his life, gaining recognition in this area later than deserved. His film music, however, was acknowledged as work of inspiration and quality early on; he wrote a number of scores for Warner Brothers in the 1930s and 1940s, including *Captain Blood* (1935), *The Adventures of Robin Hood* (1938), *The Sea Hawk* (1940) – all featuring the flamboyant actor Errol Flynn – and *Deception* (1946).

His musical style was decidedly Post-Romantic and used large orchestras to deliver sweeping melodies and grandiose gestures in the manner of the symphonic poem. The language is similar to works such as Richard Strauss's *Don Juan* (1888) or Elgar's Symphony No 1 (1907–8) – full of vitality, pathos and expression. He was highly revered in Hollywood – so much so that for *The Sea Hawk*, he was given a large budget and additional time to complete the score, and in 1938 was asked by Warner Brothers to return from Austria, where he was conducting opera, to compose the score for *The Adventures of Robin Hood*.

### The Sea Hawk (1940)

The score for *The Sea Hawk*, a film full of swashbuckling action sequences, complemented by romantic and patriotic elements, is considered one of Korngold's finest works and a masterpiece of early Hollywood sound film. It is loosely based on the life of Sir Francis Drake, set against the hostilities between England and Spain.

> The plot of *The Sea Hawk* was intended to parallel the threat posed in the 1940s by Nazi Germany: see the Queen's concluding speech.

The orchestra is a large one – 54 players plus extra Latin percussion for the Panama sequence. There are also two cues that require a mixed chorus. The scale of the musical resources is matched by the extensive amount of music featured during the film: there are only a few sections when music is dropped altogether. The role of film music in the 1940s had changed since the days of silent films, when it was used continuously throughout films. Now that films contained spoken word and diegetic sound effects, music was often considered to distract from important plot developments. However, Korngold was well known for his skill at underscoring and by this point it was accepted that a certain amount of music was necessary to enhance the emotional mood of the film and provide comment on narrative development.

The duel between Lord Wolfingham (Henry Daniell) and Captain Thorpe (Errol Flynn). Korngold writes a series of rising sequences interspersed with high trills and the excitement increases

Korngold produced a score of symphonic proportions for *The Sea Hawk*. Even the music for the opening titles suggests a full-scale operatic overture. The orchestral outpouring of emotive sweeping strings as Thorpe's ship, the Albatross, leaves Dover with Doña Maria stranded on the quayside, is typical of a style which was to be imitated by many other composers in subsequent romantic films. The reunion of the two main characters, Thorpe and Doña Maria, in the carriage towards the end of the film, presents the full versions of the main themes in order, in a kind of recapitulation, although it is very low in the mix as underscore.

The almost continuous music is full of leitmotifs; they are not used simply as calling cards, but rather are developed in a way similar to a Wagnerian music-drama. The famous fanfare played at the start of the film recurs frequently throughout, whenever there is a need to emphasise a heroic gesture or a nationalistic action (for instance, it accompanies the toast, 'serve England and the Queen').

## Korngold, 'Fanfare' from *The Sea Hawk*

The fanfare is also used in a more subtle way. For example, it announces the arrival of Thorpe in the rose garden scene, where it is played quietly on flutes to draw attention momentarily away from the rose-picking. In the first part of this scene the music is dominated by a

> There is an excellent analysis of the use of leitmotifs in *The Sea Hawk* to be found in *Overtones and Undertones* by Royal S Brown (University of California Press 1994).

leitmotif associated with Doña Maria – a sequentially treated motif made up of a rising tone followed by a perfect 4th. Here it is treated in a Ravel-like orchestration with harps and high strings. The theme is transformed as Doña Maria's carriage makes its frantic journey to Dover to warn Thorpe of the plot against him. During the journey it is given an added sense of urgency by an increase in speed, repetition and a new orchestration using brass. When Doña Maria arrives in Dover the theme is played in a lower register with a chromatic sequence, giving it a sense of dread (which is realised when she discovers the ship has already sailed).

Normally, music is written to correspond with the visuals when composers receive the final cut version of the film. However, it is worth remarking on how well the music works with the choreography of the duel between Thorpe and Wolfingham, functioning almost like a cine-ballet.

# Franz Waxman (1906–1967)

Franz Waxman

Waxman was a German Jew, but unlike Steiner and Korngold his family wasn't steeped in music and the arts. When he began his musical career he had to make ends meet playing the piano in jazz groups. He managed to break into film music by working as an orchestrator on the famous Marlene Dietrich film, *The Blue Angel* (1930). However, after being beaten up in a Berlin street, and with the Nazis in power, he fled to Paris. He then went to Hollywood, working as an arranger. His earlier creation of a successful score for a German film had impressed the English director James Whale, then working at Universal Studios on a series of horror movies, which led to Waxman's first American film commission, *Bride of Frankenstein* (1935). His highly original music for this was a departure from the classically based scores being written at the time and established him as a leading composer. The score deployed tonal ambiguity and colouristic orchestrations to build the tensions required of the genre, its most celebrated cue being the birth of the female monster. Large amounts of the music were reused by the studio for subsequent films – a testament to its quality. After *Bride of Frankenstein*, Waxman was in constant demand and in his long career he wrote the scores for such well-known films as *Rebecca* (1940), *Dr Jekyll and Mr Hyde* (1941) and *Rear Window* (1954).

His style differs a little from the composers discussed so far, although he was similarly skilled in the use of the traditional compositional techniques of motivic development and orchestration. Generally his music is less direct and he was always able to capture the subtle nuances on the screen in his music. His use of the orchestra is unique, experimenting as he did with tone colours and using string trills and tremolos impressionistically. He was also fond of creating interesting polyphonic textures and used solo instruments to great effect. He had a gift for lyricism and many of his film scores – for instance, *A Place in the Sun* (1951) and *Peyton Place* (1957) – boast highly memorable cantabile themes. The main themes from the Alfred Hitchcock romance *Rebecca* are also a good case in point.

## Rebecca (1940)

The second Mrs de Winter's (Joan Fontaine) confidence falls as she talks with Mrs Danvers (Judith Anderson)

There are a number of sinuous, flowing string themes that run through this emotional, romantic story. The film tells of a rich country gentleman (Maxim de Winter, played by Laurence Olivier) and how his relationship with a new partner is coloured by the memory of Rebecca, his late wife. Her presence permeates the

His partner is known as the second Mrs de Winter – the heroine's first name is never revealed, as it is withheld in Daphne du Maurier's original novel, to keep the focus on Rebecca.

film once they have arrived back at the family mansion (Mandelay) following a hasty wedding, and it is associated with a twisting chromatic theme, characterised by a rising or falling semitone at each bar. It makes appearances at key points in the story, such as when the housekeeper, Mrs Danvers, reminisces about her previous employer or when Rebecca's stationery is examined by the heroine. There are particular moments when the theme becomes more than just underscore, for instance when the heroine discovers Rebecca's room, preserved with all her things, and when she explores the cottage by the sea. However, it does not abruptly appear but rather is entwined with themes associated with the developing relationship between Max and his new wife. A telling passage is when Max reveals his involvement in Rebecca's death; the final scenes of the fire are also significant in this respect.

The moments of suspense and apprehension are scored using Waxman's customary skill and inventiveness. The heroine's entry into the drafty library, for example, is accompanied by tremolo strings and chromatic scales from flutes and glockenspiels, which then progresses into darker music with slow bass pedal notes as she enters the morning room (a room once frequently used by Rebecca).

A strange, electronically processed violin sound is employed in the first scene in the cottage; this returns in conjunction with a harp when Rebecca's room is revealed. The film has a large amount of underscore, which is never obtrusive but always assists in creating atmosphere and enhances the dialogue. When Mrs Danvers is in conversation with the heroine (for example, when she is explaining the gardener's telephone call), the strings are given sinking chromatic passages, which serve to draw attention to the heroine's ebbing confidence.

# 4. EPIC FILMS: HISTORICAL, ROMANCE AND WESTERNS

The characteristics of this genre can be found in productions from the earliest days of film right up to present-day blockbusters (the latter is explored in more detail on page 81). These films typically contain storylines covering wide geographical areas in the midst of intercontinental or global strife, often with historical or fantastic settings. They are usually based upon a personal viewpoint with a hero and/or heroine attempting to complete a quest, often to save the world from destruction. Large casts are involved and, in the 1950s, panoramic wide-screen sought to immerse the audience in the magnitude of the images.

## Elmer Bernstein (1922–2004)

Bernstein was a composer of many different styles and was equally at home working in jazz and pop idioms as in the more traditional large orchestral scores. His background was as a concert pianist, and he gained encouragement from the composer Aaron Copland. During World War II he produced some scores for the Glen Miller Orchestra and wrote music for service radio. He was largely prevented from writing scores for high-profile films in the early 1950s because his left-wing sympathies conflicted with the prevailing political mood of the time. Nevertheless, his exciting jazz big band score for *The Man with the Golden Arm* (1955) established him as a mainstream talent. He worked on Cecil B DeMille's film, *The Ten Commandments* (1956), and took over as principal composer after Victor Young fell ill.

His orchestral style derived from Korngold's romantic writing, with lyrical string melodies and brass fanfares, using leitmotifs to enhance characterisation or provide context for ideas. Other large-scale scores include romantic adventures such as *The Buccaneer* (1958), war films such as *The Great Escape* (1963) and *The Bridge at Remagen* (1969), and westerns, including *The Magnificent Seven* (1960), *The Comancheros* (1961) and *Hallelujah Trail* (1965). However, he was also content to work with smaller-scale scores and enjoyed using solo instruments to create intimate melodies. Two of the most well known are featured in *To Kill a Mockingbird* (1962), which uses a piano-solo theme suitable for the story of two young people set in small-town America, and *The Birdman of Alcatraz* (1962), which uses double-reed woodwind, including bassoon solos, to illustrate the subject matter appropriately. A summary of Bernstein's career should also take account of the many comedy films for which he provided scores in the 1980s: *Trading Places* (1983), *Ghostbusters* (1984) and *¡Three Amigos!* (1986), among many others. Recent work includes the score for *Far from Heaven* (2002), in which he self-pastiched earlier styles of scoring for effect.

## The Ten Commandments (1956)

The Hebrews prepare to cross the Red Sea

*The Ten Commandments* is truly an epic movie. It runs for 220 minutes and features colossal sets – recreating ancient Egypt and vistas across Sinai and the Red Sea – special effects and a cast of thousands. Such a film demands an equally prodigious soundtrack to enhance its imagery and historic themes. The unusual ploy of mimicking opera by featuring a formal overture before the producer's introduction, itself followed by the opening credits and separate accompanying music, is another indication of the scale of the film. Bernstein produced a well-integrated score, with leitmotifs for the main characters that are morphed according to circumstance. An early example of this is the use of a fanfare-like theme to represent Moses:

### E Bernstein, 'Moses' theme from *The Ten Commandments*

This motif first appears when Moses enters Egypt and Nefertiti looks down from her balcony. Note that the fanfare becomes partly diegetic as she announces that 'the trumpets tell all the world he's come back'. As the scene changes to the Pharaoh's palace the trumpeters at the door remain inactive and more fanfares are heard, yet when the music is repeated with additional drums they raise their instruments. This is a good example of the way in which music can weave in and out of an audience's consciousness. It is drawn upon in varying circumstances throughout the film as Moses's fortunes change, and is particularly telling when Moses begins to cross the desert wilderness of Sher, as the rich string textures give the theme nobility and breadth. It is even used for the opening 'curtain' music of the second half and assumes a more general function when Moses takes on the role of leading the Hebrews out of bondage.

There are a number of opportunities in the film for extended musical passages, including those provided by the sections where Cecil B DeMille, the producer, takes on the task of narrator. These include a description of the life of slaves in the brick pits, Moses crossing the desert and the gathering of the Hebrews to leave Egypt. Here the music is fully scored with yearning modal melodies in the strings that complement the fateful narrative.

The famous action passage, when the Red Sea is parted to allow the escaping Hebrews to cross to the other side, includes some of the most abiding images and impressive special effects in the film. This cue can be broken down as follows, beginning with the words 'listen to Moses, he speaks God's will':

- Stereotypical chase music with repeated-note fanfares and rising sequences accompanies the Egyptian chariots.
- Moses conjures up the pillar of fire, accompanied by music that relates to Wagner's music from The Valkyrie (1856).
- Brass fanfares and grandiose music move the scene forwards and a chorale 'religioso' is used to prepare for the parting of the waters. The music during this section is expertly mixed with sound effects and dips beneath the dialogue, which is never obscured.
- A traditional march theme is played as the Hebrews cross the Red Sea.
- The march theme is then sung 'a cappella' by the Hebrews when they are half-way across, developing into a slow chant. The removal of instruments might be seen as representing their fear of being unprotected and at the mercy of the walls of water at their sides.
- Moses ascends the rock, accompanied by a version of his original leitmotif slowed down by augmentation. He collapses the pillar of fire.
- Stereotypical chase music with repeated-note fanfares and rising sequences once again accompanying the Egyptian chariots.
- A string chorale of thanks accompanies the peace after the storm.

# The Magnificent Seven (1960)

Many westerns are produced with epic production values. The vast desert landscapes, large casts of American Indians, cavalry or bandits and often a hero with a mission make the classification 'epic' entirely relevant to this genre.

> The main theme is so memorable that it has been used whenever the Wild West needs to be hinted at, whether by film producers, commercial advertisers, rock bands or even in an episode of *The Simpsons* cartoon series.

*The Magnificent Seven* is derived from a famous Japanese film directed by Akira Kurosawa called *Seven Samurai* (1954) and transposed to a Mexican village. Bernstein's main theme is instantly recognisable with its syncopated rhythms, sweeping, high string melody and its use of the chord of the flattened seventh degree (marked with an asterisk on the score below):

**E Bernstein, Main theme from *The Magnificent Seven***

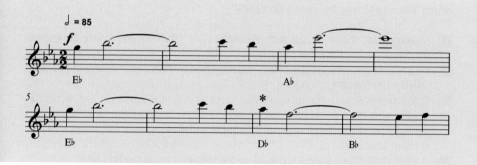

The music is influenced particularly by Copland's tone poem *El Salón México* (1932–1936) alongside other music for westerns, for instance Dimitri Tiomkin's *High Noon* (1952) and *Gunfight at the O.K. Corral* (1957).

The music alternates between two styles and sometimes cleverly combines them. On the one hand there are the cowboy-/Copland-influenced folk melodies from which style the main title music is derived: this style fits well with seven liberating gunslingers and their heroic characters. On the other, there is the Mexican music with its Spanish/phrygian influences and Latin-American dance rhythms, such as the slow bolero or tango: this is produced whenever there is a need to emphasise the rural village that is under siege, delineate its inhabitants or give extra character to the bandits. Bernstein avoided leitmotifs for characters – he could have quite easily produced a striking leitmotif for Chris Adams (played by Yul Brynner) but instead focused his music on the ethnic/geographical contrast between the different sets of characters.

The Magnificent Seven

Although a large orchestra is employed, the use of the solo Spanish guitar, in combination with various woodwind groups, also helps to create the Mexican flavour, as do various Latin-American percussion instruments. The arrival of Mexican villagers at the border town is accompanied by a slow bolero; there are dance rhythms at the villagers' training session; and for a confrontation with a bull, phrygian/Spanish chords and a scalic, high trumpet solo reminiscent of a bullfight are deployed. A slow guitar tango during the meal provides a more intimate atmosphere and the guitar is also used to good effect in the developing love scenes between Chico (Horst Buchholz) and Petra (Rosenda Monteros).

The action sequences are full of exciting timpani solos, syncopated and lombardic rhythms and dramatic orchestral effects. Bernstein produced a masterful score that further established his reputation and spawned many imitations.

# Maurice Jarre (b.1924)

From the early days of film-making, British and European films have played second fiddle – in terms of quantity, if not quality – to their American counterparts in Hollywood. The division between serious, concert-hall composers and those that wrote for films, however, was not so marked. In the UK, composers such as Arthur Bliss (*Things to Come*, 1936), William Walton (*Henry V*, 1945), Ralph Vaughan Williams (*Scott of the Antarctic*, 1947) and Arnold Bax (*Oliver Twist*, 1948) produced noteworthy scores, while in France, Honegger, Milhaud and Ibert wrote film music from the earliest days. Another member of *Les Six*, George Auric, scored numerous Ealing comedies.

> Les Six is the name given to a group of six Paris-based composers whose music is often seen as a reaction against both Wagnerian and impressionistic stylistic tendencies.

Maurice Jarre trained in Paris and wrote music for numerous French productions. However, he became internationally famous when he received an Oscar for his score for David Lean's epic production of *Lawrence of Arabia* (1962). He gained two other awards for scores written in conjunction with Lean: *Dr Zhivago* (1965) and *A Passage to India* (1984). Other scores that earned him recognition include those for Visconti's *The Damned* (1969) and Huston's *The Man Who Would Be King* (1975).

Jarre's style is very approachable and he has produced several scores where the main themes have gone on to become major popular music hits, notably the ubiquitous 'Lara's Theme' from *Dr Zhivago*. He liked to include unusual and ethnic instruments in his scores. This led to an interest in electronic instruments and the inclusion of an ondes martenot in *Lawrence of Arabia* followed his meeting with the instrument's inventor in Paris. Later scores, such as *Fatal Attraction* (1987) or the moody soundscape of *After Dark My Sweet* (1990), featured electronic music more substantially.

# Lawrence of Arabia (1962)

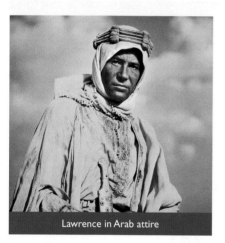

Lawrence in Arab attire

This epic production features sweeping vistas of the Sahara desert, large military manoeuvres and the progress of the redoubtable, eponymous hero. The music reflects one of the main threads of the film, that of Lawrence's gradual adoption of Arab customs, and the jaunty English march originally associated with his character doesn't survive for very long. The main tune is associated with Arabia; it is very powerful and features a falling 4th followed by a stereotypically middle-eastern rising melodic line outlining an augmented 2nd (last two notes of the second bar):

**Jarre, main theme from *Lawrence of Arabia***

The tune is highly memorable, as it is constructed in two-bar phrases. The first time it is heard (other than in the opening credits), it bursts forth at dawn in the

The cithara is an ancient instrument resembling a lyre but with a flat back. It was strung with wire and plucked with a plectrum.

desert after a very effective build-up using atmospheric tinkerings on a cithara and is then repeated in a number of guises throughout the long, unfolding adventure. Another 'Arabian' tune is featured whenever large numbers of bedouin are on the move, again stereotypical and rather reminiscent of Albert Ketèlbey's 1920 piece, *In a Persian Market*. It also makes use of augmented intervals and modal melodic outlines.

The contrast between British imperialism and Arabic nationalist hopes is, however, maintained and scenes in Cairo utilise the march *The Voices of the Guns* (1917) composed by Kenneth Alford (a composer of British army marches to rival the United States' John Philip Sousa).

Jarre creates some unnerving sounds for the tense moments when survival in the desert is the focus of the storyline. As Lawrence (Peter O'Toole) makes the dangerous trek to Aqaba, he goes back – against advice – to rescue the Arab, Gasim, who has lost his camel and fallen behind. The strength of the sun beating down is reinforced by high strings and an ondes martenot (an early electonic instrument), creating an other-worldly fear. Under this is insistent percussion with timpani and tom toms, with occasional xylophone interjections and short side-drum notes that increase in intensity as the exhausted Arab falls to the ground. The Arabian main theme is then used, communicating to the audience that Lawrence's crossing and rescue of the fallen Arab has been successful, even before he makes an appearance on screen.

# Ennio Morricone (b.1928)

Another European country producing films of merit at this time was Italy and the films of Fellini (see page 42) have become recognised classics. The spaghetti westerns of Sergio Leone were epics in their own way and the originality of Morricone's scores had a lasting effect on the styles of music which were later employed in the genre.

Ennio Morricone was a highly prolific composer, not just for westerns but for many other film genres including drama, crime and romance. He was born in Rome, and studied trumpet and composition under Goffredo Petrassi when young. He also took classes in writing for and directing choirs, and he subsequently featured various vocal combinations in his film scores. He was also a composer of concert music, and his name can be counted among other Italian composers of the avant-garde, such as Luigi Nono and Luciano Berio, although his many concert compositions haven't received the same accolades as have been heaped on his film scores.

Morricone's classical background gave him a high level of technical skill, particularly in the variety of instrumental and textural combinations that he employed, as well as in his sense of timing. *The Mission* (1986) – the soundtrack album of which sold particularly well – is notable for combining wordless chanting and hymn-like chorales, poignant solos, panpipes and percussion. He was very adept at mixing the sublime with the ridiculous: a light-hearted or banal pop theme might be made to contrast with a deeply moving passage of religious fervour, for instance in *Two Mules for Sister Sarah* (1970).

His famous scores include *Days of Heaven* (1978), *The Untouchables* (1987) and *Cinema Paradiso* (1988). However, the films he scored for Sergio Leone, including *A Fistful of Dollars* (1964) and *The Good, the Bad and the Ugly* (1966) remain his most widely recognised and celebrated compositions.

### The Good, the Bad and the Ugly (1966)

The three gunslingers face each other in a 'Mexican standoff'

This film is an epic western where the tale of three bounty hunters is set against the backdrop of the American Civil War. The main motif in the score is made up almost entirely of rising and falling perfect 4ths (A–D–A–D–A). The motif occurs with slight alterations in three versions, as if each phrase represents one of the three characters, before it concludes with a fourth, balancing phrase. We first hear it during the opening credits, and each phrase is scored differently (whistling, vocalising and tuned percussion) to further differentiate 'the good', 'the bad' and 'the ugly', and the phrases reappear throughout the film when one particular character is foregrounded. The link is confirmed in the closing shots of the film.

The theme is so memorable that it was turned into a huge popular music hit in a band arrangement by Hugh Montenegro in 1968.

**Morricone, *The Good, the Bad and the Ugly***

Overall, the film demonstrates a number of key features of Morricone's style, particularly for westerns:

- Male chorus shouts
- Electric guitar themes
- Percussion
- Harmonica and trumpet solos.

A passage worth noting is the section where 'the ugly' is being beaten up by 'the bad' in a prisoner-of-war camp; while outside, a diegetic, sweet-sounding waltz is rendered by a prisoners' ad hoc instrumental group. While the guard at one point exhorts them to play more sweetly, the music is juxtaposed with the violence inside the cabin.

Finally, the extended periods of silence which build up tension – particularly during close-up shots or duels – and explode into music at key dramatic moments, should be mentioned. When the Union army storms the bridge and the battle scene commences, while other composers may have deployed grandiose music, here, there is only the noise of the guns: Morricone reserves the music for the three main characters. The classic three-way gunfight at the end is enhanced by an accelerating obbligato theme which stops and starts, a high trumpet solo, paso doble rhythms and choral dorian-mode harmonies.

# 5. DRAMA, MYSTERY AND SUSPENSE

This section will look at some examples of films that fit within a broad spectrum of genre types. Drama normally refers to films that focus on problems or the interactions between individuals or small groups in real-life situations – social problems, civil rights, law courts and political intrigue all feature in this genre. Mystery and suspense movies concentrate on the thrills or danger generated by the plot rather than concentrating on the figure of the gangster, detective or oppressed heroine. It is how the characters come into conflict with outside forces that is important.

## David Raksin (1912–2004)

While Raksin was not as prolific as some of the previously mentioned composers, he worked in Hollywood as an arranger and orchestrator for a considerable period, and his B-movie and TV music output is substantial. He started his work arranging Charlie Chaplin's original themes for the film *Modern Times* (1936), which used a synchronised soundtrack but no dialogue. It was the film *Laura* (1944) that brought him to international attention but, despite its commercial success, it was his two later films which earned Raksin Oscar nominations: *Forever Amber* (1947) and *The Bad and the Beautiful* (1952). He was not afraid to experiment with musical styles and devices, and his scores were daring for their time, full of chromatic melodic twists and unusual-time signature changes. *Forever Amber* is notable for its neo-classical counterpoint, but it is his most famous film, *Laura*, that we will examine more closely.

### Laura (1944)

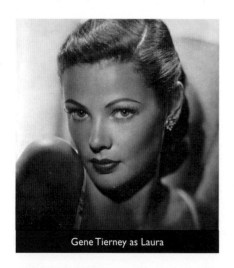
Gene Tierney as Laura

This intriguing 'whodunnit' is concerned with a heroine, presumed dead, and a detective who falls in love with her. Her presence runs throughout the film, right from the appearance of her name in the title sequence to the fact that she is the topic of most of the conversations. This is considerably enhanced by the music. A chromatic jazz melody (shown on the right) is played so often, and in so many different circumstances, that it comes to haunt the listener, and the brevity of other thematic ideas is such that the film can be thought of as mono-thematic.

**Raksin, 'Laura's theme' from *Laura***

Raksin avoids the possibility of tedium, which the extensive use of this theme could create, partly through the melody's unusual line and associated jazz-based extended harmonies, and partly by never stating the theme in its entirety. Even the fully orchestrated version played with the opening credits misses out its last phrase and concludes with a hanging pivot note to take the viewer into the first scene. After that, until Laura makes her appearance the tune is most frequently used diegetically – on a gramophone, in a restaurant played by an instrumental combo of violin, accordion and piano, and at a party in a version for dance band. When Laura returns, fuller versions of the theme are heard non-diegetically, but the same arrangement is never heard twice. When the audience leaves the cinema the tune goes with them. Understandably there were many popular music arrangements of this tune and *Laura* was the first film to achieve widespread commercial success through the record sales – by various artists – of its main theme. Later, it became more common for studios to exploit the soundtracks of their films to increase revenue.

One final aspect of David Raksin's adventurous scoring should be mentioned. In the scene where the detective is searching Laura's apartment, a processed piano sound is used, created by uneven bearings on the tape machines and by judicious mixing techniques. This represents a very early use of electronic sound processing and shows Raksin's more experimental side.

# Miklós Rózsa (1907–1995)

Born in Budapest, Rózsa always felt he owed much to his native country and the influence of Hungarian music. The classical composers Bartók (1881–1945) and Kodály (1882–1967) were influenced by Hungarian folk music, whose modal and tritonal scales can be traced in the composers' works. Miklós Rózsa started out imitating their style with a series of concert compositions. However, after moving to Paris and meeting Honegger he was persuaded to try his hand at writing for films. In pursuit of this goal he moved to London and started writing music for London Films – a production company run by fellow Hungarian Alexander Korda.

In 1939 he moved to Hollywood, where he scored over 100 films. His success was reflected in several awards – for the nerve-jangling Hitchcock thriller *Spellbound* (1945),

*A Double Life* (1947) and the big-budget epic *Ben-Hur* (1959). Other epic films which he produced scores for include *Quo Vadis* (1951), *El Cid* (1961) and *The Golden Voyage of Sinbad* (1974).

## Double Indemnity (1944)

An uncertain love affair

Written in the same year as *Laura*, this is an even darker film noir based on an insurance swindle and a murder. Throughout the film there are sections narrated by the lead character Walter Neff (played by Fred MacMurray) as a voice-over. This is typical of the film noir style, and both personalises the story and adds to its sinister side. The following musical themes are associated with ideas and functions rather than specific characters:

- **Fate and doom** – the opening material with its insistent, slow timpani beats; this makes several reappearances, particularly to emphasise the failure of Neff's hopes
- **The forward motion of the plot** – functioning as a kind of ritornello and link to the narration; this is represented by strings with repeated, fast-moving quavers
- **Love theme** – used for the uncertain love affair between Neff and Phyllis (Barbara Stanwyck).

All three of these themes are in a minor key, although the love theme has some major key moments. However, Rózsa's avoidance of the sharpened seventh makes the themes more modal than tonal. He develops them symphonically, extending and inverting them melodically and crafting them into extended cues, such as the murder sequence or the depositing of the body on the railtrack. He uses the full studio orchestra to good effect, with pounding brass and timpani to build tension. One particularly telling moment in the closing scene is when a solo violin emerges from the orchestral tutti as Neff finally collapses.

> The sharpened seventh is the interval between the first and last notes of the scale and is responsible for the music being in a key, or having a tonality. Without this the music sounds modal.

This film set the standard for film noir in the 1940s and Rózsa produced several scores in the same style. However, by the time he left Paramount Studios for MGM in 1949, his interest lay with scoring for epic films.

# Bernard Herrmann (1911–1975)

Bernard Herrmann was born and raised in New York. As a young man he was a fan of Charles Ives (1874–1954) and later adopted some of this progressive composer's techniques. While chief conductor of the CBS Symphony Orchestra, he introduced more new music to the American public than any other conductor.

His early success as a composer came working in radio with Orson Welles, and when this famous actor and producer moved to RKO to work on films, Herrmann followed him. Here he wrote the score for *Citizen Kane* (1941), often cited as one of the most important films in cinema history. Musically, the film is notable for the close collaboration between director and composer, a rare occurrence then and now.

In the 1950s and early 1960s he worked with Alfred Hitchcock on many gripping suspense films, including *Vertigo* (1958) and *North by Northwest* (1959). He also collaborated with Oskar Sala, producing the electronic soundscape for *The Birds* (1963). This film has no music and the noise made by the birds, assumed to be natural and diegetic, is actually artificial and is the only soundtrack. Herrmann used electronic instruments in other scores, notably the theremin in *The Day the Earth Stood Still* (1951), and was willing to depart from

> The theremin is an electric instrument, named after its Russian inventor, Léon Theremin, that is controlled by hand movement, but without touching the antenna and metal loop which make up the instrument.

the symphony orchestra commonly used by studios and utilise interesting sound combinations. He used five organs in *Journey to the Center of the Earth* (1959) and the music for *Fahrenheit 451* (1966) – written when he moved to England – is scored for two harps, vibraphone, xylophone and glockenspiel.

His musical style avoids lyrical melody, concentrating on motifs and ostinato patterns. Often, motifs assume importance through their rhythmic treatment. The music is coloured by interesting chromatic harmonies and instrumental combinations. The author Royal S Brown identifies a minor triad with a major seventh as a chord commonly used in Herrmann's Hitchcock films – and the interval of a 3rd used as a vertical building block to be characteristic traits of his musical style.

## Psycho (1960)

This famous film score embraces many of Herrmann's skills as a composer for the moving image and constitutes a landmark in the history of cinema. Its unusual strings-only orchestration runs counter to the normal Hollywood assumption that strings should primarily be used for lyrical romantic themes. With its single tone colouring, the score reinforces the black and white visuals of the film. Throughout the film Herrmann exploits the versatility of the violin family to the full, exploring contrasting textures and utilising instrumental techniques such as pizzicato and glissando.

Ostinato patterns are used extensively throughout the score. Herrmann repeats motifs made from pairs of rising semitones and adds stabbing rhythms in the lower strings to maintain long cues of heightened tension. As the anti-heroine Marion Crane (Janet Leigh) drives through the rain the insistent rhythms of the score correspond with her growing anxiety. Above this rhythmical music the violins play a more sustained contrapuntal scalic motif, which rises and falls, first from a B♭ then a tritone lower, from an E. Nerves are set on edge!

The knifeman attacks

The famous shower scene where Marion is knifed to death makes use of high strings playing augmented octaves with stabbing down-bows. The added reverberation makes the sound truly terrifying and the scene, visually horrific though it is, would lose much of its potency if the sound were to be omitted – a fact belatedly acknowledged by Hitchcock, who commissioned the music for this particular scene later than the rest of the score. After the murder, an eerie atonality is maintained as Norman Bates (Anthony Perkins) clears up the now vacant room.

Indeed, the generally chromatic language of the score often avoids a tonal centre, seeming content to create musical motion though techniques such as inverted and retrograde melodic lines, octaves and semitone trills. Augmented chords and tritones add to the tonal ambiguity.

# Nino Rota (1911–1979)

This talented Italian composer came from a musical family and carried out his early musical studies in Milan. He moved to Philadelphia in 1930 for two years to complete his studies in orchestration and composition, afterwards returning to Italy. Throughout the 1940s he scored a large number of Italian films and in 1952 began a fruitful partnership with the renowned director Federico Fellini. Among the many films Rota scored for Fellini are *8 1/2* (1963), *Roma* (1972) and *Amarcord* (1973). His last film with Fellini was *Orchestra Rehearsal* (1979) – of particular interest to musicians, depicting as it does a difficult relationship between a German conductor and an Italian orchestra.

Rota also wrote music for several Shakespeare productions, most notably *Romeo and Juliet* (1968), directed by Franco Zeffirelli. However, it is his music for *The Godfather* (1972) and its two sequels, directed by Francis Ford Coppola, that ranks as one of his finest achievements. The lyrical Romantic style he employs is tonally based, but influenced more by Smetana than Rachmaninov, alongside Rota's role model Copland and, of course, the 19th-century Italian school.

## The Godfather (1972)

This film suits Nino Rota's musical style perfectly. Although it is set in 1940s New York and is full of brutal gangster violence, the real interest lies in the film's human element. Consequently, Rota's score is composed of lyrical melodies and subtle menacing underscore, as well as source music which is used in the scenes depicting weddings and other social gatherings. The family life of the members of the central Italian mafia gang (the Corleones) is enhanced by music that captures their homeland of Sicily.

Two main themes dominate. The first is played unaccompanied at the very start of the film by a solo saxophone and is made up from winding semitones and a falling 3rd (a falling 4th on the phrase's repeat). This theme appears repeatedly to represent the Corleone family. When the action moves to Sicily half way through the film another important theme is introduced, this time based on a rising G minor triad, and an implied falling tritone. The theme is played by tremolando mandolins and, after the film's release, became a huge musical hit for the studio. Both themes maintain a melancholy minor mode, reflecting the tragic development of the plot.

Marlon Brando and Al Pacino in *The Godfather*

**Rota, The Sicilian love theme from *The Godfather***

The use of music in the baptism scene near the end is worth noting. The organ music, attributed to Bach, is manipulated in such a way as to enhance the contrasting cut-aways of the series of murders. While these are inserted into the cathedral scene, the music, the sound of the priest and the baby remain continuous, and the minor and diminished harmonies add significantly to the tension.

# Thomas Newman (b.1955)

This ground-breaking composer belongs to a film-scoring Hollywood dynasty which includes his father, uncle and brother – all film composers – and his cousin Randy Newman, a singer/songwriter. He has won a number of awards for his work, which often makes extensive use of electronics, tuned percussion and samples. A good example of this is the soundtrack for *American Beauty* (1999), which won several awards, incorporating a number of popular songs in contrast with the looped, gamelan-sounding original music.

For films such as *The Shawshank Redemption* (1994) and *Road to Perdition* (2002) he used a more conventional orchestra, but the textures and harmonies employed are no less innovative.

## The Shawshank Redemption (1994)

Newman created a soundtrack for this tense prison drama that predominantly uses strings playing sustained lines over which pianos or other percussion add an extra dimension of rhythmic and melodic interest. Harmonies are sometimes quite discordant and do not necessarily follow traditional functional progressions.

He is fond of using contrasts, not just of timbre but sometimes overlaying completely different pieces, in the manner of Charles Ives. One example of this is the opening. The song played under the credits, an old Inkspots number called *If I Didn't Care*, gradually becomes diegetic as its tone quality loses its lower partials, sounding more like a car radio. The scene focuses on Andy Dufresne (Tim Robbins) who is handling a gun. Gradually, Newman's music is mixed in – it is sustained and tense, clashing with that of the Inkspots and adding to the surreal, anxious atmosphere. The film cuts to a courtroom where Andy is on trial, and the music is heavy with ominous timpani rolls and a piano evoking tolling bells. The scene then cuts back to the car, where the Inkspots are warbling against Newman's doom-laden music.

Among the many cues worth examining is one near the end of the film. A full orchestra is employed as Andy makes his escape from prison, with a four-note Stravinskian ostinato breaking into a climactic major chord as he cleanses himself in the falling rain.

Scene from *The Shawshank Redemption*

# 6. COMEDY

While comic films can be divided into several sub-categories, including slapstick, satire, black, situation and romantic comedy, their music soundtracks often share common qualities:

- A light character, avoiding serious symphonic moods, except when used ironically
- A tendency to repeat material (familiarity can be a source of humour)
- Familiar formulas taking sudden, surprising turns
- A fast tempo (slow music is used only occasionally, for instance in scenes of pathos)
- Certain instrumentations which conjure amusement (for instance, the stock unaccompanied bassoon phrase)
- Exaggerated 'mickey-mousing', particularly in slapstick scenes.

# Roy Webb (1888–1982)

Roy Webb began his career as a conductor on Broadway, specialising in directing musicals by Richard Rogers. He worked with Max Steiner at RKO and went on to become their musical director in 1936. During the 1940s he scored a number of suspense movies for the company, for which he employed advanced harmonies and melancholy themes. He gained a reputation for his ability to conjure up 'big city' ambiences in his sound world, which were particularly suited to film noirs (*Stranger on the Third Floor*, 1940; *Murder My Sweet*, 1944; *The Spiral Staircase*, 1945).

However, his familiarity with popular styles and his ability to write a good tune brought him many light comedy and romantic films to work on, and he received Academy Award nominations for seven of these. He is widely credited for developing the click track.

> The click track is a kind of audio metronome used for synchronisation purposes. Also credited for its invention are Carl Stalling and Max Steiner. From 1967 the more sophisticated SMPTE time code was used.

### My Favorite Wife (1940)

*My Favorite Wife* is a classic example of a screwball comedy: it has a central romantic plot, which is thwarted by a series of mishaps and misunderstandings. Nick Arden (Cary Grant) is shocked to see his first wife, Ellen Arden (Irene Dunne) – who has been missing for seven years – after he has remarried, and he tries to conceal her existence from his new bride.

Cary Grant in *My Favourite Wife*

The music score is present in the film only when it needs to be. It begins with a waltz featuring a sweeping string section and a memorable tune that recurs later in the film, as a motif to signify romance. Webb uses light orchestration, which, at certain points, follows the action closely in a cartoon style. When Nick arrives in the hotel with his new wife, his first wife, Ellen, looks on from the lobby and we hear a darkened version of 'Here Comes the Bride', prefiguring the trouble to come. This is followed by a rising string-and-oboe figure to enhance Ellen's hopeful anticipation of seeing her husband again. As the newlyweds enter, they are accompanied by a falling solo piano, echoed by strings and clarinets, and as they approach the hotel desk we hear a comic bassoon solo.

Webb resorts to 'mickey-mousing' on occasions throughout the film. The sliding trombones as the lift door closes at the end of the above scene is an example of this. After a long period in the middle of the film when there is no music, there is a slide note on timpani when an insurance agent informs Nick that his first wife has been alone with another man on a desert island for seven years. The treatment of 'Jingle Bells' at the end of the film, where the rhythms are dotted, is also an example of comic musical transformation.

# Henry Mancini (1924–1994)

After World War II Mancini worked as a pianist and arranger with the Glen Miller Band under its new director, Tex Beneke (Glen Miller had died in a plane crash in 1944). This gave him a lifelong love of jazz, which is reflected in many of his scores. When he initially began working at Universal Studios in 1952 he worked primarily on sci-fi and horror movies (such as *Creature from the Black Lagoon*, 1954; *It Came from Outer Space*, 1953; *Tarantula*, 1955; *This Island Earth*, 1955). The studio decided to do a biographical film entitled *The Glen Miller Story* (1953) and Mancini was the obvious choice to work on the soundtrack, for which he subsequently achieved an Academy nomination.

As the big studios gradually disbanded during the 1950s, Mancini was well placed to work as a freelance composer and arranger. He produced a large body of work for writer and producer Blake Edwards, including *Breakfast at Tiffany's* (1961), *Days of Wine and Roses* (1962) and *The Pink Panther* (1963).

His musical style combines orchestral scores containing nostalgic melodies (for instance, in *Charade*, 1963) with jazz and popular elements, rarely using atonal techniques. Consequently many of his theme tunes have been re-recorded and have achieved a life of their own beyond the films. Famous examples include the song 'Moon River' and the instrumental 'Peter Gunn'.

## A Shot In The Dark (1964)

Peter Sellers as Inspector Clouseau in
*A Shot in the Dark*

This was the second in the *Pink Panther* comedy series, featuring the bungling French police inspector, Jacques Clouseau (Peter Sellers). Mancini employs two main themes throughout the movie. The first to appear is an exaggeratedly romantic, stereotypical French ballad, entitled 'The Shadows of Paris'. It is in a nostalgic, minor key and is sung with passion. It is performed as underscore to the long opening as various lovers creep around between hotel rooms in the dark, its contrasting mood adding a satirical, comic aspect to their actions. Later appearances of the theme are often played on an accordion. It often accompanies romantic situations, whenever Clouseau is offering his 'protection' to Maria (Elke Sommer).

The opening credits are followed by a 'detective' theme, which provides much of the music in the film. It features an ostinato pattern played on electric guitar, reminiscent of a *Bond* score, with a blues melody over the top. This appears whenever Clouseau is attempting some 'clever' detective work. A comic aspect is introduced by sudden cutting, firstly to a clip from Offenbach's 'Can-Can' and then to a short excerpt from the 'Shadows of Paris', coinciding with Mancini's name in the credits.

This most famous version of the can-can is actually the 'Infernal Gallop' from Offenbach's opera, *Orpheus in the Underworld (1858)*.

# Ira Newborn (b.1949)

Newborn has written scores for many modern comedies, based on the wacky or parody comedy genres. Particularly successful are the films from the *Naked Gun* series (1988, 1991, 1994), *Police Squad!* (1982) and *Ferris Bueller's Day Off* (1986). He was also musical director and producer for *The Blues Brothers* (1980). His characteristic style favours blues and rock but he has wide-ranging tastes. He is currently professor at New York University in the Department of Music and Performing Arts.

### Ace Ventura: Pet Detective (1994)

For this anarchic film the director, Tom Shadyac, combines Ira Newborn's original scoring with imported commercial singles, including 'Mission Impossible', 'The Crying Game' and 'The Lion Sleeps Tonight', all used in a satirical way, to provide an extra comic dimension.

Newborn's original score is used in two main ways. Firstly, the big-band, driving rock music, with heavy improvised electric-guitar lead parts, blaring brass and saxophones, underscores many of the car chases and provides excitement and an ironic exaggeration of Ace Ventura (Jim Carrey)'s capabilities. The sexy saxophone lead for the police chief is also given an ironic dimension by the revelation, at the end of the film, that 'she' is in fact a man. Secondly, Newborn writes dramatic underscore for various suspense scenes, utilising strings and vibes (see, for instance, the scene at the killer whale's tank or approaching Ray Finkle's house). He blends jazz funk with some of this traditional writing as the situation changes, for example in the hospital's storeroom as Ventura fears he is going to be discovered. A celestial female chorus is employed effectively when his hidden animals emerge in the flat at the start of the film, and to create atmosphere when he visits Ray Finkle's bedroom.

# 7.  WAR FILMS

This genre, although applicable to all human conflicts, is – in terms of both Hollywood and British cinema – mostly comprised of narratives from the two world wars of the 20th century. There is sometimes a moral message built into the plot, often about what is seen as the futility of war, and although large forces and special effects are important the more personal human problems of broken love affairs or family displacement are often foregrounded.

## Malcolm Arnold (1921–2006)

This British composer of concert music wrote the music for several films, including *Hobson's Choice* (1954), *Bridge on the River Kwai* (1957) and *The Inn of the Sixth Happiness* (1958). His style was more lyrical than his contemporaries Britten and Walton, and much more tonal than many of the European classical composers of the time, and so he was naturally suited to writing music for films destined for mass consumption. His abilities as a composer of major works (he wrote nine symphonies and 20 concertos, as well as operas and ballets) make him an important figure in 20th-century music, and he brought many of his skills to his film scores.

### The Bridge on the River Kwai (1957)

Arnold's score for this gripping saga set in a Japanese prison camp contains only a small amount of music. The atmosphere is largely created by the natural sounds of the jungle environment, sometimes with added effects. Apart from a few short dramatic moments, there are no lengthy cues until almost an hour into the film, when the American prisoner, Shears (played by William Holden), makes his escape down-river. The action music is chromatic, based on rising melodic sequences, and designed to support the visuals rather than lodge itself in the viewer's memory.

However, earlier in the film a company of British soldiers captured in Singapore enter the camp whistling the main theme from Kenneth Alford's regimental march *Colonel Bogey*. Clearly this is diegetic music. However, Arnold picks up this march and uses it cleverly throughout the film, blending it with a melody of his own, based on the same harmonies. The various arrangements of this famous tune reflect the changing fortunes of the prisoners. At the end, any patriotic triumphalism would be inappropriate, so the *Colonel Bogey* march is withheld and it is Arnold's own march that concludes the narrative.

## Dmitri Tiomkin (1894–1979)

Tiomkin was an accomplished concert pianist from the Ukraine. When he moved to the United States in 1925 he was torn between composing and performing, but a broken bone in his hand decided his career for him. His use of American folk song, with its pentatonic melodies, and the employment of a lyrical and largely tonal language make his music instantly accessible. It proved to be eminently suited to westerns and his score for *High Noon* (1952) – for which he wrote the hit song 'Do Not Forsake Me, Oh My Darlin' – confirmed his position as the first-choice composer of this genre. However, he did not restrict himself to westerns: his grandiose style was similarly suited to films such as *The Guns of Navarone* (1961) and *The Fall of the Roman Empire* (1964), which inspired him to compose big scores, although his music was usually orchestrated by others. It would be a mistake, however, to assume Tiomkin's music was stylistically predictable: witness the film *Cyrano de Bergerac* (1950), in which he employs a range of styles from pastiche French Baroque to modern idioms.

## The Guns of Navarone (1961)

David Niven, Gregory Peck and Anthony Quinn in *The Guns of Navarone*

This wartime epic is set on the Greek islands and tells the story of a band of intrepid saboteurs with a mission to destroy some strategic German guns. Tiomkin makes no attempt at writing Greek music for underscore, preferring instead to use ethnic diegetic music to enhance the celebratory atmosphere of a wedding. The score would suit any dramatic narrative. It centres upon a single identifiable theme, pentatonic in outline and used in a wealth of variations to suit the particular situation. It is transposed into the minor key for dangerous situations, and is contracted, extended or re-orchestrated for underscore. It remains, however, essentially heroic and is fully realised in the closing sections when the team are laying explosives to sabotage the guns.

### Tiomkin, *The Guns of Navarone*

The German forces are dehumanised by having a solo snare drum playing a military rhythm associated with them. Music is used sparingly but to great effect in some of the most exciting scenes; for example, in the scene when the team is scaling the cliffs in severe weather, the natural sounds of the storm provide the soundtrack, but music cuts in when Captain Mallory (Gregory Peck) slips and is saved from falling by Colonel Stavros's grip.

# Wojciech Kilar (b.1932)

This composer belongs to the Polish avant-garde movement of the 1960s, which includes other luminaries such as Krzysztof Penderecki (b.1933) and Henryk Górecki (b.1933). He wrote orchestral and chamber music together with a substantial amount of film music, mostly for Polish productions. From the mid-1970s he worked in Hollywood, particularly for the director Roman Polanski.

### The Pianist (2002)

Kilar contributed important underscore to this film in which the classical music of Chopin, together with short passages of Bach and Beethoven, play a central role. Non-diegetic music begins when the wall surrounding the Nazi-established Jewish ghetto in Warsaw is erected. This sustained, minor-key string music occurs in other scenes depicting the Jewish community. When Wladyslaw Szpilman (Adrien Brody) finds himself alone after his family have been forcefully taken away on the trains, a poignant solo clarinet theme appears. This is used several times, representing his loneliness and despair.

It is, however, the piano music which gives the film its overall unity. Sometimes it is clearly diegetic – as when Szpilman plays Chopin's Ballade Op 23 no 1 (1835–6) to the sympathetic German officer – while at other times it is conjured in Wladyslaw's mind (when Wladyslaw practises the piano without touching the keys, for fear of discovery, we hear the melody that is playing in his head), so although strictly non-diegetic, it does still exist within the world created by the film. A passage from Beethoven's 'Moonlight Sonata' (1801) is used to great effect when Szpilman explores the devastated buildings, yet it is unclear whether the music exists in his mind or only in ours.

The pianist (Adrien Brody) at the piano

# 8. ANIMATION

There are two main types of animated film:

- Cartoon comedy shorts and dramatic action-hero series, mostly written for television, with a varying degree of animation
- Full-length feature cartoons with full animation or stop-motion models.

This book will concentrate on feature films, while acknowledging that much of the technical groundwork was developed by the shorts.

Animation directors are not usually musical and there are some instances in the early days of animation when the composer would write the music before the animator even began work. This was only short-lived, however, and composers were soon given a 'detail sheet' that indicated the action, dialogue, sound effects and precise timings. They still composed without seeing the film, although sometimes were lucky enough to be given a black and white rough cut called a pencil reel.

It was expected that the music would mimic every small movement of the animation, reinforcing or illustrating the action. This technique was called mickey-mousing. One problem composers faced was that in order to synchronise the sound and vision they had to work to a click track. This meant that anything that wasn't completely metrical – rallentandos and pauses for example – was difficult to incorporate. Also, although the music utilised a regular metre, some of the hit points were anything but on the beat. Furthermore, the music had a very short time to make its point. The common musical style adopted for live action films in Hollywood at the time was Post-Romantic, but this was not suitable for animation. Composers adopted the more structured neo-classical compositional techniques and borrowed ideas from opera buffa, although these were deployed at a more hectic pace.

# Frank Churchill (1901–1942), Leigh Harline (1907–1969) and Larry Morey (1905–1971)

This team of composers wrote for the Disney studios in the 1930s. Churchill began as a silent movie pianist and moved to Disney in 1930, scoring many animated shorts such as *Three Little Pigs* (1933), which included the hit song 'Who's Afraid of the Big Bad Wolf?'. This changed the way Disney studios viewed music for cartoons. He also worked on *Peter Pan* (1953), *Dumbo* (1941) and *Bambi* (1942). Churchill worked with Larry Morey to produce a series of hit songs for Disney's *Snow White and the Seven Dwarfs* (1937), and produced the main instrumental score, together with Leigh Harline.

## Snow White and the Seven Dwarfs (1937)

Snow White and the Seven Dwarfs make music together

This film was a landmark in the history of animation: it was the first full-length feature cartoon and used full animation techniques, including a rotoscope (in which drawings are taken from live-action movement). In essence, it is an animated musical, featuring such hit songs as 'Someday My Prince Will Come', 'Heigh-Ho' and 'Whistle While You Work'. True to the prevalent style of the 1930s and 1940s, the music plays almost continuously throughout the film, so the underscore produced by Churchill and Harline represented a substantial piece of work. Its constituent parts include:

■ Light music in the style of popular musical comedy of the time
■ Dramatic action sequences that combine Max Steiner influences with classical music, such as Dukas's *Sorcerer's Apprentice* (1897) (see the chase scenes and the music for the wicked queen)
■ Development of the hit songs' thematic content, in a dance-band style or orchestrally, often corresponding to the dance sequences
■ An innovative style of music related to recitative, in which the music directly imitates speech (see Snow White's identification of the cleaning jobs in the cottage)
■ 'Mickey-mousing' to complement characters' movements – a technique often seen in cartoon shorts of the time.

Churchill, 'The Dwarfs Approach Their Cottage' from *Snow White and the Seven Dwarfs*

The orchestrations and textures are particularly noteworthy. For the most part they are light, so as to avoid overpowering the dialogue. Typical scorings include the use of pizzicato strings, piccolo and glockenspiels. The comedy tortoise is, stereotypically, assigned a bassoon. Dance-band sequences involve muted brass, woodwind and strings reminiscent of British bands of the period, such as those directed by Lew Stone and Henry Hall.

# Louis Febre (b. 1959)

This talented composer/arranger was born in Mexico in 1959 and trained in Los Angeles. He came to prominence after receiving an award for the score he co-composed for the TV series *The Cape* (1996–7) with John Debney. He had a box office success with *Swimfan* (2002) and was nominated for an Annie Award for his music for the direct-to-video animated feature film *Scooby Doo and the Alien Invaders* (2000). Other television work includes the soundtracks for *Smallville* (2001–) and *Desperate Housewives* (2004–).

### Scooby Doo and the Alien Invaders (2000)

This film is a modern-day feature-length production based on the long-running TV series that began in 1969. Like the TV series and other cartoons from the Hanna-Barbera stable (for example *The Flintstones*, or *Yogi Bear*), the animation is simplified and stylised. However, unlike shorts, which tend to rely on library-style stock cues and underscores rather than entirely original material, there are few shortcuts made with the music in this film.

Louis Febre produced a score that drew the best from contemporary blockbusters. Full orchestral tuttis are employed for the sci-fi subject matter, with grandiose chords based on augmented harmonies to suggest the awe of outer space, ominous, slow, bass lines for danger, and harp glissandi plus strings for eeriness. One interesting touch is the use of an upward violin slide to imitate the theremin, a sound to send shivers down your spine. The score uses mickey-mousing to a restricted degree, usually in the slapstick action sequences. A favourite mickey-mousing technique is used to accompany the fright of discovery, whenever a character is surprised from behind by a scary alien: a loud, dissonant chord is held for a second before dissolving into scurrying, fast semiquavers, accompanied by sound effects as the character flees.

Another convention of the *Scooby Doo* series was to use pop-like songs at key points in the narrative. This is picked up in the feature-length film, an example being the love scene between Shaggy and Crystal where a soft rock song entitled 'How Groovy' (Bodie Chandler) is used as underscore. Even the title song, 'Scooby Dooby Doo, Where are You?' (Mook and Raleigh) is incorporated into the film and used for the first alien chase.

# Michael Giacchino (b.1967)

Giacchino came into film from the world of video games. In 1997 he wrote the score for *The Lost World: Jurassic Park* – the first video game to use a live orchestra. He has gone on to compose orchestral scores for many more video games, including a number set in World War II, such as *Medal of Honor* (1999) and *Call of Duty* (2003).

In 2001 he moved into television (he composed scores for *Alias* (2001–6) and *Lost* (2004–) – the latter famous for its use of percussive sounds derived from plane fuselage) and then into feature films, with his 2004 animated feature *The Incredibles*. His recent achievements in animation soundtracks include the Disney features *Ratatouille* (2007) and *Up* (2009).

### The Incredibles (2004)

The animation for this tale of a superhero family uses 3D computer graphics to produce realistic action sequences, although the characters are still exaggerated cartoon figures. The music uses powerful, driving, big-band conventions, derived from the spy-movie soundtracks of John Barry, but with a modern orchestration: high brass sections that produce tightly rhythmic stab chords, saxophones and lots of percussion – including xylophone and timpani – are the main instrumental forces.

For the most part Giacchino avoids mickey-mousing. The animation is treated as if it were a live-action feature film, the music track adding atmosphere and enhancing the action. However, there are a few moments when the soundtrack follows the action more literally. Here is a brief analysis of the music that accompanies Elastigirl's efforts to penetrate the enemy stronghold, beginning at the point when she is wrapped around the door:

1. Stab chord as sliding doors trap her leg
2. 'Walking' quavers
3. Crotchet triplet augmented triads as she reaches for the key
4. Slide down and thump as she fails
5. 'Hey!', then crash chords as she hits the guards
6. Semitone high trill to maintain tension
7. Another hit
8. Further walking quavers for stuck leg
9. Crash chord and muted brass progression for car trip
10. Final crash chords as she defeats guards.

The music written for the exciting chase through the jungle and the closing fight with the robot monster are further testament to Giacchino's considerable skill as a film-music composer.

# Danny Elfman (b.1953)

Danny Elfman had little formal musical training, but through his enormous talent and imaginative approach he has produced a body of original work that is the envy of many a Hollywood composer. He worked first with his brother, a rock musician and film producer (*Forbidden Zone*, 1980), and then with Tim Burton, a director who shared a similar vision to Elfman, with an interest in subject matter on the dark, gothic and weird side.

After the success of *Beetlejuice* (1988) the director/composer team moved on to bigger projects. The big-budget movie based on the super hero *Batman* (1989), which is also produced with gothic noir imagery, has a large orchestral score. Elfman uses a five-note motto for Batman (C–D–E♭–A♭–G, transposed down a semitone for the opening titles), whose music remains mostly in the minor key. As a quirky contrast, the music for his antagonist The Joker is often in the major. One of the most inspirational sections of the soundtrack is the waltz (to the death) danced by The Joker and Vicki Vale on the top of the cathedral. Elfman has a love for triple-time music, particularly when he can use it in an ironic situation.

> See *Danny Elfman: Batman in Focus* by Mark Wilderspin (Rhinegold Education, 2007).

For the fairytale *Edward Scissorhands* (1990), Elfman uses some subtle, impression-istic, yet eerie music which has subsequently become widely copied in the industry. The team have produced two major animation features, both based on stop-motion puppetry and with a virtually continuous music score: *The Nightmare Before Christmas* (1993) and *Corpse Bride* (2005).

### The Nightmare Before Christmas (1993)

This film functions as an animated musical. It is a tour de force of musical imagination and visual animation, only equalled in effect by its sequel *Corpse Bride* (see the cover image). The opening chorus of 'This is Halloween' sets up many of the stylistic features to follow. The music is in a jaunty, duple time, scored for an eclectic orchestra that includes strings, muted brass and tuba, tubular bells, chinese blocks, xylophone and banjo. Vocal lines are often in parallel but at least two octaves apart. For this Stravinskian pot pourri of timbres, Elfman uses the extremes offered by the instrumental registers. For Jack's first song (in triple time) a celesta and solo saxophone add further colour.

When Jack arrives in Christmastown he sings a song that encapsulates much of Elfman's style – 'What's This?'. It is quick, scored lightly with contrasting timbres; it moves between D♭ and C major, and is constructed from highly irregular phrase lengths – three $\frac{3}{4}$ bars precede two $\frac{2}{4}$ bars of melodic extension, which catapult the listener into the two bars of $\frac{2}{4}$ that introduce the next verse:

## Elfman, 'What's This?' from *The Nightmare Before Christmas*

Jack Skellington in *The Nightmare Before Christmas*

# 9. HORROR, SCI-FI AND THE SUPERNATURAL

These films are designed to take us out of the real world and play on our worst night-mares. They utilise the power of fear to create entertainment, catalysing our imaginations with special effects and fantastic visions. Not surprisingly, the soundtrack, combining music and sound effects, makes a critical contribution to the film's ability to produce the required audience reaction.

## Jerry Goldsmith (1929–2004)

Goldsmith's music covers a wide range of styles, a substantial period of time (his career spans 1957–2004) and a variety of innovative approaches. This prolific composer received lessons from the Italian émigré Mario Castelnuovo-Tedesco – who had a reputation for a delicate and refined style – and from the more traditional film composer Miklós Rózsa (see page 38). He began his musical career in television, where his improvisation and continuity skills were tested nightly, playing the music for the live TV suspense series *Climax* (1954) using a piano, organ and novachord (an early Hammond synthesiser). Consequently he learnt how to make music both economical and effective, a skill he soon applied successfully in the film industry.

For fantasy, sci-fi and horror films Goldsmith created effects that sounded electronic. However, he drew upon orchestral resources – acoustic instruments, or instruments that have been processed electronically but can still be played in 'real time'. Examples of films that feature this technique include *Alien* (1979), *Hollow Man* (2000) and *Poltergeist* (1982), and favourite devices include extreme instrumental ranges, string glissandi and harmonics, brass mutes and percussion effects. The wide spectrum of compositional techniques used by Goldsmith draws parallels with classical composers such as Stravinsky, Bartók, Berg and Debussy, but he drew greatest inspiration from contemporary film composers such as Alex North (1910–1991) and John Williams (b. 1932) (see page 81).

> In *Chinatown* (1974) he deploys the unusual combination of strings, four pianos, four harps, a solo trumpet and percussion.

### Planet of the Apes (1968)

This sci-fi film is set on a planet where apes are the dominant life form. The soundtrack reflects this alien environment, utilising atmospheric scoring with an abundance of percussion. Goldsmith employs ethnic instruments such as a ram's horn and various African drums, to imply the tribalism of the ape society, as well as for the purely sonic qualities they offer. He also uses effects processing to transform his sounds: for example, reverberation is added to xylophone notes and the bass flute is put through a kind of electronic harmoniser.

A highly chromatic motif is used, to emphasise the alien nature of the film's subject:

### Goldsmith, chromatic motif from *Planet of the Apes*

The opening three notes of this (a descending minor 3rd and a rising semitone) are found throughout the film as a motto theme. The score contains little that could be described as melodic. It is mainly atonal in character, reflecting the central character, Taylor (Charlton Heston)'s feelings of frustration and entrapment. Twelve-tone motifs are embedded within the score, such as in the excerpt from 'The Hunt' below:

### Goldsmith, 'The Hunt' from *Planet of the Apes*

Low-pitched piano stabbing chords and disjunctive violent phrases abound and the action moments often evoke Stravinsky's *The Rite of Spring* (1913) or the same composer's neo-classical orchestral pieces that include piano (for instance, his Symphony in Three Movements, 1942–5). Bartók's Sonata for Two Pianos and Percussion (1938) is also an influence, but Goldsmith's music is even more violent than this, using the extremes of instrumental registers and severe dynamic contrasts.

The hunt scene

### The Omen (1976)

Goldsmith held strong convictions about the role music should play within film:

'I think sometimes you can have too much music. I'm probably more conservative about it than anybody; I don't want to write more than is absolutely necessary. *Patton* had 33 minutes of music, and the movie was two and a half hours long'

(*Knowing the Score,* D Morgan, Harper Entertainment 2000).

There are many examples of the telling use of silence throughout Goldsmith's films. When, in *The Omen* (1976), Robert Thorn (Gregory Peck) and the photographer arrive in the Italian monastery, short phrases of music are punctuated by gaps, enabling the chanting of the monks to rise to the surface and enhance the overall atmosphere of the scene. In a cue later in the film, as Robert moves towards Damien (Harvey Stephens) to cut his hair (to ascertain whether he bears the incriminating '666' birthmark), the musical atmosphere is tense. Low strings creep in, accompanied by piano tone clusters.

> Tone clusters are formed when a number of adjacent notes are sounded simultaneously.

A motto theme – a falling 6th (G–B♭) – is developed throughout the film, acting almost as a leitmotif for the Thorn family and its steady disintegration. There are gradual transformations of the theme, both melodically and instrumentally. Contrast, for example, the version of the theme played during the bedroom scene, towards the beginning of the film – when Robert and Katherine (Lee Remick) share their anxieties about Damien with one another – with the version played later, when Katherine lies in her hospital bed. Here, the theme sinks chromatically, ending on a flute flutter-tongue, underscoring the words 'kill me'. Similarly, when Katherine announces her pregnancy and her desire for an abortion, a much darker version of the theme is used.

The other important motif in the film is, of course, the demonic 'Sanctus, Daemius', which uses repeated Bs. This repeated, quasi-religious chant is enhanced by church bells and, later in the film, by drums to build tension, becoming more forceful and insistent to match the increasing tension of the plot.

Goldsmith's use of tonal contrast is also worth noting. The shift from the hesitant, chromatic harp music towards the beginning of the film, when Robert is in the convent, to the sunnier, major tonality when he presents the newborn baby to his wife is typical of the composer's skill in subtle musical transformation. Again, after Damien appears to be lost by the river and is subsequently found, the scene shifts to a birthday party where a music box is playing 'Happy Birthday' in an uncomfortably unrelated key. The use of a Haydn string quartet (Op 3 no 5, second movement) as source music is also an inspired contrast to Goldsmith's frightening cue for Damien's panic attack in the church.

# John Carpenter (b.1948)

Generally speaking, there have been few instances in the history of cinema when a film's director and its music composer have collaborated closely with one another. Rare examples include the Russian director Eisenstein, who worked with Prokofiev on *Alexander Nevsky* (1938), and Orson Welles, who adapted his shots to correspond with the music of Bernard Herrmann in *Citizen Kane* (1941). In the case of John Carpenter, however, the relationship between film direction and music composition could hardly be closer as, for many of his productions, this imaginative director composed his own musical scores.

> John Carpenter has not scored the music for all of his films, however; Ennio Morricone wrote the score for *The Thing* (1982), one of Carpenter's best-known films.

Carpenter's preference has been for horror and suspense movies, and his scores usually involve a solo piano set against synthesisers and electronic effects. Well-known films for which he directed and composed music include *Assault on Precinct 13* (1976), *Halloween* (1978), *The Fog* (1980) and *Vampires* (1998).

### Halloween (1978)

The opening music for this so-called 'slasher' movie contains all the basic ingredients of the simple but effective score:

**Carpenter, opening music from *Halloween***

There are various themes that occur whenever suspense is required. Most feature the interval of a semitone:

- Ostinato quavers as in the above theme played on piano (above)
- Rising minor 3rd and falling semitone in the bass

- Consecutive harmonic minor 2nds, falling by step, again on piano

- Slower quavers moving by repeated falling semitones

- Held minor 2nds on high synthesised strings.

These themes are developed sequentially downwards, extended, or played in various combinations. Even just a single note, using the same timbre, is enough to create a fright – when Annie Brackett is murdered in her car, for example.

No new musical material is introduced until the closing chase scene between Myers (Tony Moran) and the heroine Laurie Strode (Jamie Lee Curtis), when a repeated, insistent bass piano note suddenly appears, impelling the action forwards.

Sound design in general plays a crucial role in *Halloween*. The sound of Myers's heavy breathing and the unsettling sounds of the night add an extra layer of tension to a film that manages to maintain an almost constant level of suspense throughout.

# Vangelis (b.1943)

This Greek composer worked in London for 12 years in a studio full of electronic equipment and percussion instruments. His film soundtracks explore the sonic landscapes which can be created with analogue synthesisers, sound-processing equipment and overdubbing techniques. In his early career he worked in progressive rock bands and went on to produce a number of solo electronic music albums. He achieved international recognition as a composer of film music, winning numerous awards for his electronic score for *Chariots of Fire* (1981) set in the Paris Olympics of 1924. Following on from this he produced the haunting score for the cult movie *Blade Runner* (1982), working with director Ridley Scott, with whom he also produced music for the New World historical adventure *1492: Conquest of Paradise* (1992).

## Blade Runner (1982)

Vangelis created a highly atmospheric soundtrack for this sci-fi movie, set in a dark, industrial future. Much of it uses layered textures, created by the large collection of synthesisers in his studio, together with some processed percussion sounds. The music is improvised to produce melodic fragments over sustained chord progressions. The harmonies used are largely triadic and the melodies often move by step. Chromaticism is reserved for the relationships between one chord and another, for instance a D major chord moving to an A♭ major one. In other words, the harmonic language is often restless, avoiding perfect cadences and traditional modulations, slowly morphing from one chord to another using link notes or pivots. Most of the time it is non-functional.

> Non-functional means that, rather than chords moving from one to another following hierarchical, tonal relationships (tonic, dominant and so on), they are chosen simply for the emotional or sonic effect they produce when juxtaposed.

The futuristic environment in *Blade Runner*

Common harmonic progressions in Vangelis's music include:

- Minor to relative major (e.g. D minor to F major)
- Minor to tonic major (e.g. A minor to A major)
- Mediant relationships (chords whose roots are a major or minor 3rd apart e.g. C major to E major)
- Parallelism (chords moving in blocks up or down e.g. G major, F major, Eb major)

- Chords changing over or around pedal notes (e.g. C major moving to D major while the bass note stays on C)
- Tritonal relationships (chords whose roots are an augmented 4th apart (e.g. F major to B major).

At other times the harmony is static. One minor chord will be sustained using a synthesised string-like sound, and sound effects or single notes are layered over this chord, like points of light in a dark sky.

> Technically, this string-like sound is known as a 'pad'.

Similarly, melodic lines gradually evolve as scenes progress, becoming longer and more meandering. The rate of harmonic change within these extended themes is slow. On other occasions Vangelis repeats a fragment of melody, perhaps just a falling tone, harmonised in 3rds (for example in the 'Wounded Animals' cue) while other musical events change. Sometimes, single notes feature a downward glissando, producing a sighing effect. These motifs act as a binding agent to give the music unity and also an element of wistfulness or nostalgia, which corresponds to characters' recurring uncertainty about whether their past life is real or manufactured.

> One important and recurring motif is the huge reverberated bass drum sound which represents the futuristic cityscape.

However, there are certain cues in the film when Vangelis resorts to a more traditional musical language. One of these is the cue when Deckard explains to Rachel that her memories are implanted. A distant solo piano gradually makes its presence felt, featuring a gentle, falling 4th motivic introduction, which then evolves into a flowing theme in D major, based on traditional progressions.

# Dane Davis (b.1957)

Davis had a traditional musical education, after which he worked with small jazz ensembles, performing and arranging. He came to film composition after working extensively in television in the late 1980s and early 1990s. He was employed in Hollywood as an orchestrator on films such as *Bound* (1996), which led directly to his recruitment as the composer for the sci-fi blockbuster *The Matrix* (1999) by the film-making brothers Larry and Andy Wachowski. This was a huge box-office success and spawned two major sequels.

Davis's compositional style is distinctly modern, employing jazz, dance and avant-garde influences and avoiding overtly sentimental lyricism.

### The Matrix (1999)

Set in an existentialist future in which humans are controlled by machines, *The Matrix* is reminiscent of *Blade Runner* in its dystopian vision. There are also similarities between the soundscapes produced for both films; like Vangelis, Davis avoids traditional orchestration and thematic development. However, while the music for *Blade Runner* belongs to the analogue age, *The Matrix*'s score is thoroughly digital, corresponding to the futuristic technology depicted in the plot. There are no identifiable musical themes, the main material consisting of a combination of music samples and sound effects. However, the score gains an internal unity through the consistency with which these are deployed.

The many action sequences feature crashing, reverberant orchestral stabs, fast-moving bass lines and screechingly discordant high notes. Sometimes, brass sounds are employed for a sense of grandeur, as well as techno music, notably in the nightclub scene near the beginning of the film and in Neo's (Keanu Reeves') and Trinity's (Carrie-Anne Moss') attack on the security building, in their attempt to rescue Morpheus (Laurence Fishburne). The diegetic track, 'I'm Beginning to See the Light', played when Neo goes to meet the Oracle, seems particularly appropriate.

See www.filmsound.org/danedavis/

The score has been much imitated, to varying degrees of success. Sound designers and mixers are always important in films, but in *The Matrix* this is particularly true. Specific mention should be made of the extensive sound design of Dane Davis and his ProTools/MetaSynth studio, as well as the music mixer, Dave Campbell, who worked initially with six orchestra and six synthesiser tracks provided by the composer. These two personnel were key to the soundtrack's success.

ProTools and MetaSynth are professional-level software programs, often used in recording studios.

# 10. ROMANCE, ACTION AND ADVENTURE

Films that can be categorised as belonging to the romance genre include romantic comedies, tragic love stories and even filmed stage musicals. There are very few films that do not contain some human pathos, often manifested as a love affair, while action and adventure films are romantic in the sense that they place an emphasis on heroic achievement or are set in exotic locations. Many of the films that we have already mentioned would easily qualify as romantic, such as *Laura* or *Lawrence of Arabia*. The films that we shall consider in this chapter, however, have a particularly strong claim to be considered in a survey of the genre.

It was a common trend in Hollywood to follow up a successful formula with another similar film, and this certainly applies to many screen romances. Examples of famous pairings in films include Humphrey Bogart and Lauren Bacall, Spencer Tracy and Katharine Hepburn, and Rock Hudson and Doris Day. We will begin, however, with a British film by David Lean – the archetypal tear-jerker *Brief Encounter*.

### Brief Encounter (1945)

In *Brief Encounter* the director David Lean decided he would use Rachmaninov's Piano Concerto No 2 as his soundtrack. It is not unknown for a film director to plunder the classical repertoire, and of course this was common in the silent film era. What is rare is for a single work to be used quite so systemically.

> Sergei Rachmaninov (1873–1943) was a Russian composer who emigrated to America in 1918. His lush, late-Romantic orchestral style was hugely imitated in the film industry.

The visuals that accompany *Brief Encounter's* opening credits show a steam train passing by a station platform. The black and white photography employs dark lighting and the opening of the piano concerto – with its heavy, tolling minor chords – contributes to the sombre atmosphere and signals the fateful events to come. The bittersweet story of a chance meeting in a railway station waiting room, seemingly prosaic, is elevated by the couple's dreams of a life together, enhanced by the inherent pathos of the music. The solo horn melody of the second movement is used for thoughtful moments when Laura Jesson (Celia Johnson) is daydreaming. Rachmaninov's melodic style employs twisting, chromatic sequences that pull on the heart strings. The sustained string melody, accompanied by slow, arpeggiated piano chords, is used extensively to enhance moments of intimacy between the illicit lovers (she is a married woman). The third movement scherzo is used for cues that involve action and the maestoso final theme plays alongside the husband and wife reunion. When a gramophone is played in the Jesson's living room, the music of the concerto is used diegetically, yet functions non-diegetically as well. The director fades in the various cues with a profound understanding of the relationship between sound and vision.

# Leonard Bernstein (1918–1990)

As a composer, conductor and pianist, Bernstein was a major force in American musical life. He had a unique understanding of the relationship between drama and music, and wrote several highly successful stage works, including the ballets *On the Town* (1944) and *Candide* (1956) and his most famous work, the musical *West Side Story* (1957). He worked extensively in television and lectured on musical analysis. He employed a modern compositional language, derived in part – as so often – from Bartók and Stravinsky, which he combined with his love of jazz and Latin-American music to produce a powerful, rhythmic, harmonically rich and tellingly melodic style. His single feature-length film soundtrack is a noted masterpiece.

### On the Waterfront (1954)

This love story is set against a background of mob violence and corruption in a New York dockland. Highlights of the music include:

■ An unaccompanied horn melody based on rising minor 3rds, representing the industrial landscape, complemented by a ship's foghorn that echoes across the landscape:

**Bernstein, opening music from *On the Waterfront***

■ Barbarous driving rhythmic passages, with repeated motifs employing timpani, drums and piano for violent scenes
■ Stabbing brass chords against chromatic string ostinatos, notably in the church storming scene
■ Huge orchestral tuttis that exploit the sonic capabilities of the instruments
■ Motto theme comprising a falling semitone and perfect 4th, used in a variety of orchestrations and tempi to provide wistful moments or an aggressive action theme
■ Lyrical, sustained underscore on strings and/or solo flute for love scenes
■ Shostakovich-influenced pounding timpani and brass for Terry Malloy's (Marlon Brando's) walk to lead the men to work in the closing scene
■ Diegetic jazz mood music.

# Michael Kamen (1948–2003)

This American composer studied the oboe before going on to a career in rock and pop music. He worked in cross-over classical-rock styles but then moved on to arrange music for a number of groups, including Pink Floyd, Queen and Eurythmics, as well as solo artists such as David Bowie, Sting and Kate Bush. His film-music credits include *Brazil* (1985), *Highlander* (1986), *Lethal Weapon* (1987) and *Robin Hood: Prince of Thieves* (1991).

He won a British Academy TV Award for his score for the series *Edge of Darkness*, which he wrote in collaboration with Eric Clapton. Despite his rock background he tended to write orchestral underscore for his action films, leaving the idiomatic rock music to others, or working on it in cooperative ventures.

### Robin Hood: Prince of Thieves (1991)

For this action-packed blockbuster, Kamen produced a traditional orchestral score in the manner of Korngold. The various fight sequences utilise heroic brass fanfares which follow the action closely (thereby employing a degree of mickey-mousing) and characteristic march-like music to represent Englishness. There are, however, darker passages – for example when the Sheriff consults the evil witch Mortianna (Geraldine McEwan) – when lines become more chromatic and orchestrations more impressionistic, using low basses, synthesised ringing, and voice-like sounds and textures, which are widely spaced to suggest the underground dungeon. The song that Bryan Adams wrote for the film ('Everything I Do, I Do It For You'), based loosely on a musical phrase from Kamen's score, was sung under the closing credits and became a massive hit in its own right. This encouraged other producers to request that hit singles be included somewhere in the scores for their films.

# Hans Zimmer (b.1957)

Like Kamen, this German-born composer started his career in popular music. However, he worked predominantly with electronic resources, collaborating with bands such as Ultravox, with whom he pioneered the first use of computers on stage. Nowadays Zimmer is best known for his efforts to blend electronic sources with orchestral scores. During his early career in film he was based in London, working closely with prolific film composer Stanley Myers, on films such as the *The Deer Hunter* (1978), one of his best-known scores. Zimmer's big breakthrough was his award-winning score for *Rain Man* (1988). He proceeded to win an Oscar for his score for the animated feature *The Lion King* (1994) and later produced his most widely recognised music for *Gladiator* (2000). Other notable successes include *Thelma and Louise* (1991), *The Prince of Egypt* (1998), *The Last Samurai* (2003) and the two most recent films in the *Pirates of the Caribbean* series (2006 and 2007).

His compositional style typically employs modal harmonies and pulsating electronic bass lines, sonorous brass sections, choirs and sometimes metallic-sounding electronic crashes. The dark brooding scores of *Backdraft* (1991), *Crimson Tide* (1995) and *Gladiator* are representative of this approach.

## Gladiator (2000)

Maximus (Russell Crowe) encourages his troops before the battle in Germania – the beginning of an exciting orchestral cue

Perhaps influenced by the invaluable knowledge he gained when Stanley Myers acted as his mentor, once he was successful, Zimmer decided to invite a number of young composers to work with him. One of these was the imaginative vocalist Lisa Gerrard, who produced the quasi-Celtic/Arabic melismatic vocals that permeate the score of *Gladiator*, adding tremendously to the atmosphere. These were improvised over sustained pedal notes and are used as a leitmotif to represent the romantic ideal of a pastoral home life, distant and inaccessible.

The music for the battle in Germania at the beginning of the film is highly exciting, manufactured from repeated, short, chromatic motifs with pounding brass and drums, evoking Shostakovich's symphonic allegros. Several of the main

> The technique of introducing variations or fragments before the main statement of a theme is heard was pioneered by Sibelius.

themes are related tonally and melodically, being based on aeolian harmonies (utilising a chord which has the flattened seventh degree as its root), often in a chorale-like form. One of these makes a telling appearance at the close of the battle, when its noble melodic line emerges through the clashing of swords as the action is rendered in slow motion. It is a variant on a theme used later in the film to represent freedom. This theme re-emerges at moments of high emotion and is used at the end of the film when it develops from Gerrard's improvisations for the cue 'Now We Are Free'.

**Zimmer, 'Now we are Free' from Gladiator**

There are clear Wagnerian influences to be heard when the new emperor, Commodus (Joaquin Phoenix), makes his triumphal entry into Rome (suggestions of the gods entering the newly-built Valhalla in Wagner's opera *Das Rheingold* (1869) perhaps?). However, alongside such full orchestration, Zimmer is also capable of employing highly reduced scorings. For the underscore accompanying the scene in which Commodus tells his sister, Lucilla (Connie Nielson), and her son, Lucius, how the emporer was betrayed, single notes are held for long periods of time. For the cue 'Am I Not Merciful?' (when Commodus tells his sister she is to provide him with an heir), weaving string lines are heard, in the style of the Polish composer Górecki.

The film is notable for the sheer quantity of music. Interestingly, though, the two most important fights in the coliseum, between Maximus (Russell Crowe) and the tigers, and between Maximus and Commodus, rely on sound effects only.

# Dario Marianelli (b. 1963)

This Italian-born composer has won a number of awards for his scoring of films adapted from novels – particularly *Pride and Prejudice* (2005) and *Atonement* (2007) – both of which utilise the English Chamber Orchestra and the renowned concert pianist Jean-Yves Thibaudet. He has also written several successful scores for films located around the world in Asia and Africa.

### Atonement (2007)

Marianelli's score for this adaption of Ian McEwen's best selling 2002 novel brings the interplay between diegetic and non-diegetic sound to a new level of sophistication. Right from the start, the film title appears on the screen as if typed and the authentic sound of a 1938 typewriter accompanies it. We move into the bedroom of Briony Tallis (Saoirse Ronan) where she is busy typing up her first play. She rises from her seat to take the manuscript to her mother but the typing sounds remain as a percussion sound in the non-diegetic score. Throughout the film these sounds are used to remind us of her, or of the consequences of her actions. A few notes are sounded when she falsely accuses Robbie Turner (James McAvoy) of rape, which leads to a triple time waltz created from the keys and the carriage return. Later scenes of nurses at a wartime hospital as they march purposefully down the corridor are accompanied by typewriter sounds which alert us to Briony's presence amongst them.

Other examples of this interaction are:

- The sound of a bee on a window counterpoints with strings in the soundtrack
- A plucked grand piano string on-screen is perfectly in tune with the non-diegetic rippling piano in the score
- A group of soldiers at Dunkirk sing the hymn 'Dear Lord and Father of Mankind' in the same key as a sustained orchestral string chorale, with the differing harmonies creating an emotional poignancy.

A haunting motif appears in a number of guises throughout the first section of the film, creating a sense of tension (see below) and a more traditional sweeping string love theme reaches its full realisation at the end of the story.

**Marianelli, *Atonement***

Briony (Saoirse Ronan) clutching her first play, as Robbie (James McAvoy) approaches

# 11. MUSICALS

After the success of *The Jazz Singer* (1927), the first commercial film to synchronise sound with images, there was an influx of composers and arrangers into Hollywood and the public developed an appetite for sound films which incorporated musical numbers. This was later met with a backlash, as audiences began to feel that music hampered important dialogue. Eventually audience opinion swung the other way, however, and there were a series of big productions by Busby Berkeley where the sheer ambition of the musical productions carried the day.

It should be noted that songwriters are treated differently from the composer of the film's underscore. They are involved from the beginning and have to have their songs composed and recorded before filming can begin so that the actors can lip sync to camera.

There are three main types of musical film:

- A film that has had musical numbers written for it. These might be written by the composer of the underscore, in which case there is likely to be some degree of integration and consequent artistic unity. Examples of this type of film include *Top Hat* (1935), with music by Irving Berlin, and *Beauty and the Beast* (1991), a Disney animated feature with score and songs by Alan Menken.

- A film that has had previously existing numbers inserted into it for either artistic reasons or, more commonly, for a possible financial boost. Sometimes the film company owns a music production company and can import a popular song directly from their own catalogue. Either way, a music supervisor is employed to manage copyright and if necessary re-record the track.

  Films that are not musicals have also adopted this approach: *Midnight Cowboy* (1969) had the ballad 'Everyone's Talkin' at Me', sung by Harry Nilsson, added (although John Barry, the composer of the score, was allowed to edit it).

  Examples of this type of film include *Singin' in the Rain* (1952) – most songs written by Nacio Brown and appearing in earlier films – and *The Blues Brothers* (1980).

- A stage show or operetta that has been transferred to film. There are considerable advantages to transferring tried and tested work onto the screen. A film production can have more ambitious sets than are possible on stage, use camera close-ups to capture facial expressions and can generally be more enterprising when it comes to sound-mixing. Inevitably, however, the excitement of live stage action is reduced somewhat. Examples of this type of film include *The Wizard of Oz* (1939, music by Harold Arlen), *Cabaret* (1972, music by John Kander) and *Evita* (1996) from Andrew Lloyd Webber's smash West End hit.

More details on specific musicals can be found in *Musicals In Focus* (2nd edition) by Paul Terry (Rhinegold Education, 2009).

# 12. DOCUMENTARIES

This type of film concentrates on factual descriptions, or reports of a non-fictional nature, and musical accompaniment is very much dependent on subject matter. Most documentaries are made for television and producers are understandably wary of using music in the background of reports. For example, in a report on a Middle-Eastern conflict or a political conference, music would supply an unwelcome emotional input that would colour the dispassionate information-giving.

However, historical documentaries might use music of the period to engage the audience and add an additional realistic dimension to the narrative. Similarly, nature films delivered simply as factual reports can lose the interest of the viewer and so music can be used to help dramatise the images and commentary. The BBC is renowned for its series of nature programmes, and few of their producers avoid music altogether. One exciting passage which is worth studying, from the many filmed from Peter Scott onwards, is the battle between ants and termites in David Attenborourgh's *Life in the Undergrowth* series (2005), with music by Ben Salisbury and David Poore.

> *Nanook of the North* (1922) – credited as the first anthropological documentary – was a silent film about the life of an Inuit. It had soundtracks composed separately for it in 1947 and 1976 by Rudolph Schramur and Stanley Silverman respectively.

In terms of feature films, the highest grossing nature documentary to date has been *March of the Penguins* (2005). The frozen wastes of the South Pole and the emotional story of the penguin colony are perfectly complemented by Alex Wurman's sweeping orchestral score, featuring sustained and moving string parts, lyrical woodwind solos, minimalistic piano and tuned percussion loops.

## Bruno Coulais (b. 1954)

Parisian Bruno Coulais began his career as a classical musician and moved into film and television in the late 1970s. His work in the following decade was mostly in television and film shorts, including documentary soundtracks. International success arrived when the nature documentary *Microcosmos: le peuple de l'herbe* (1996) won numerous awards and made him one of the most sought-after composers in French cinema. The vocal content of his scores for films such as *Himalaya* (1999) – with its blend of ethnic instruments from Nepal and Buddhist chant – and *Les Choristes* (2004) – exploring the effects of choral singing on juvenile delinquents in a depressing boarding school – considerably enhances the impact of the narrative. Mystery and suspense films such as *Les Rivières pourpres* (2000) also benefit from his skills of matching music to dramatic situations and he has written for French blockbusters such as *Belphégor - le fantôme du Louvre* (2001). As his career progressed he continued to produce documentary soundtracks, such as that for *Winged Migration* (2001).

Coulais employs a musical style that is inventive and creates atmosphere with innovative textures and instrumentation. His language is sometimes atonal, but frequently chromatic or

73

based on a tonal centre, with a subtle, original style of phrasing. He enjoys using the human voice, often as a colouristic effect, and sometimes mixes in electronic sound sources.

## Microcosmos: le peuple de l'herbe (1996)

Snail love in *Microcosmos*

This seminal nature documentary is particularly useful for musical analysis as there is no voice-over commentary. Using cutting-edge photography, the film shows close-ups of small creatures (including pond life) in a meadow, at various times of day and in varying weather conditions. Flowers opening and grasses growing are captured in slow motion.

There is a surreal atmosphere, helped to a great extent by Coulais's imaginative score. This employs percussion (both tuned and untuned), vocal solos from a boy treble and a mezzo-soprano, strings and fuller orchestral sounds mixed with electronic effects, and real-life (actuality) noises created, for example, by insect movement.

Highlights from the numerous music cues include:

- 'Microcosmos' – the title track, featuring tuned percussion and boy treble (the composer's son), considerably influenced by Danny Elfman's music for *Nightmare Before Christmas* (see page 58) and including chromatic harmonies, particularly minor triads shifting down a semitone
- 'The Bee and the Flowers' – string special effects and percussion are mixed with the bees' buzzing wings
- 'The Ladybird' – pizzicato strings mirror the fussy movements of the insects
- 'Spiky Caterpillars on the March' – timpani and percussion give a powerful lead to the movements
- 'Snail-love' – features mezzo-soprano and orchestra, reminiscent of *Songs of the Auvergne* by Canteloube (1879–1957)
- 'Dung Beetle' – orchestral march portraying the confident rolling of the ball of dung, which collapses into musical chaos as the ball gets impaled on a twig.

# 13. ART FILMS

Sometimes known as arthouse, this genre defines films that have high artistic values, and avoid commercialism. They often carry a message such as criticism of government or society, or simply explore the philosophical relationship between sound and vision. They are aimed more at a niche market, often showing in festivals and speciality theatres. Notable artistic experimental films include: the films of Luis Buñuel, Ingmar Bergman and Jean Cocteau, Satyajit Ray's *The Apu Trilogy* (1955–1960), François Truffaut's *The 400 Blows* (1959), Jean-Luc Godard's *Breathless* (1960), Werner Herzog's *Aguirre, the Wrath of God* (1972), Alan Parker's *Pink Floyd The Wall* (1982), the films of the British director Peter Greenaway and Krzysztof Kieslowski's *The Double Life of Véronique* (1991).

European art film, unlike films made in the USA and Bollywood in India, is often government-funded. It includes such movements as German Expressionism, Italian Neo-Realism and French and Eastern-European New Wave.

## Michael Nyman (b.1944)

Nyman studied at the Royal Academy of Music and King's College London, where he was a pupil of Thurston Dart, before working as a music critic and performer in the early 1970s. He produced a large number of film scores for the director Peter Greenaway, including *The Draughtsman's Contract* (1982), *Drowning By Numbers* (1988) and *The Cook, the Thief, His Wife and Her Lover* (1989). He had a major commercial success with his soundtrack for *The Piano* (1993), and has also composed a considerable body of work outside the film industry.

> Thurston Dart (1921–1971) was a British musicologist, conductor and keyboard player, specialising in early music.

His compositional style exists within the minimalist school – music based on repeated fragments, often in a tonal idiom but not necessarily following functional harmonic progressions.

> Nyman is, in fact, reputed to have coined the term 'minimalism' himself in 1968 in an article in The Spectator about the composer Cornelius Cardew.

### The Draughtsman's Contract (1982)

The elegant draughtsman

Set in an English country mansion in 1694, the story tells of a draughtsman employed to create a series of drawings of the house from different angles. The music reflects the draughtsman's geometric approach. It is almost exclusively based on a series of ground basses by the English composer Henry Purcell (1659–1695) over which Nyman adds his own melodic developments, employing syncopation, suspensions and rhythmic ingenuity. 'An Eye for Optical Theory' was thought to be by Purcell but was subsequently discovered to be based upon a ground bass by William Croft (1678–1727):

**Nyman, ground bass used in 'An Eye for Optical Theory' from *The Draughtsman's Contract***

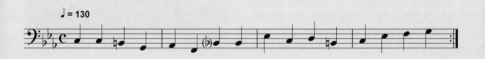

# Philip Glass (b.1937)

This innovative American composer has been influenced by eastern philosophy. He studied at the Juilliard School of Music in New York and with Nadia Boulanger in Paris, and has composed operas, symphonies and chamber works. His music for film includes *Koyaanisqatsi* (1983) and *Powaqqatsi* (1988), which examine the relationship between humans and the environment, *Mishima* (1985), *Kundun* (1997) and *The Illusionist* (2006). He also scored the 1931 film *Dracula* in 1999.

He is very interested in the relationship between sound, vision and the audience, striving in his scores to provide listeners with a way in to the film and dislikes allowing too much to be dictated by the film-makers. Like Nyman, Glass is often grouped within the minimalist school, however he prefers to be known as a composer of 'music with repetitive structures' rather than as a minimalist, writing lyrical, melodic phrases that twist and turn, creating a weaving texture.

### Koyaanisqatsi (1983)

The opening sequence establishes the film's concerns. Images of cave drawings by Hopi Indians are contrasted with a slow-motion sequence of a rocket launch. This section is scored for organ, with a repeated basso profondo D (almost two octaves below middle C). This is followed by an aerial view of a rocky desert, while strings hold long notes. Further images of the natural world are presented using footage that is either slowed down or sped up and the music becomes increasingly complex, with ostinato arpeggios creating hypnotic motion.

We move, via a quarry, to power stations and nuclear tests, and 23 minutes into the film we see human figures for the first time. Glass, appropriately, deploys choral music at this point. As the visuals focus more on urban activity the music becomes even more complex, eventually reaching a climax, followed by silence. Images of a cityscape are followed by urban decay and night traffic, and the music builds again. Eventually, after a sequence where the rocket launch fails, we are returned to the cave with a recapitulation of the opening music – the suggestion is that life is now out of balance (the film's title is a Hopi word meaning 'life in turmoil').

There is no dialogue in the film; unity of music and vision is achieved, while providing an audience the opportunity for reflection, as both Glass and the director Godfrey Reggio would have intended.

Cityscope in *Koyaanisqatsi*

# 14. MODERN BLOCKBUSTERS

A blockbuster is a big-budget movie that has high production values but, in order to recoup the immense investment involved, also generates associated commercial enterprises through music (CDs and downloads) and memorabilia (for example, action figures). Frequently there is much media hype before the release of the film, with news and internet previews, music tracks being released, and interviews with the big stars. The subject matter and cast members are chosen to have a wide appeal and composers employed are likely to have a proven track record.

## John Williams (b.1932)

This highly successful and gifted film-music composer wrote the soundtrack for the first recognised blockbuster, *Jaws* (1975). He has gone on to write music for many of Stephen Spielberg's other blockbusters such as *Close Encounters of the Third Kind* (1977) and *Jurassic Park* (1993), and also worked with George Lucas on the *Star Wars* and *Indiana Jones* series and with Richard Donner on *Superman* (1978). All these films had sci-fi and/or fantasy story lines, but John Williams has also scored films with a more human focus such as *The Paper Chase* (1973), based on a law school, and *Schindler's List* (1993), a film set during the holocaust with music of hauntingly beautiful, melodic pathos.

His technique involves a largely traditional use of the orchestra (he was resident conductor of the Boston Pops) for underscore, in the manner of old Hollywood masters such as Steiner and Korngold, treating the audience to aural feasts of richly scored fanfares, battle music, triumphant marches and soaring love themes. He uses an accessible tonal harmonic language but is willing to extend this to use impressionistic or atonal techniques when the dramatic moment requires. After the smaller-sized combos of the 1960s and 1970s, or the synthesised, sampled music and experimental instrumentations of the 1980s, John Williams is credited with popularising the traditional use of the orchestra.

### Jaws (1975)

This terrifying movie, set in a small seaside resort, concentrates on the attacks of a great white shark on the bathers near the beach. Williams uses various orchestrations to enhance the underwater scenes, employing harps, ominous double basses, horns and bass clarinet, and high string harmonics for tension. There are a number of important minor-key themes, such as the business-like fugato when the protective cage is being built, or an expectant rising horn call including a tritone, but the main theme – associated with the shark itself – is Williams's real tour de force.

This theme, that simply uses a repeated rising semitone in the bass, creates real fear whenever it is played. It starts slowly and gradually builds as the danger approaches, and is only used when the shark is actually there. Various false alarms on the beach do not trigger the theme – viewers know when the shark is a present danger simply by the music.

The composer uses his orchestral forces carefully. The full brass section is sav
for the closing scenes and the double-bass sonority is used to evoke watery depth;
a peaceful, rocking, Sibelius-influenced horn motif closes the action as the two men
paddle to shore, and to safety.

### The Empire Strikes Back (1980)

Darth Vader

ckbusters

busters

film to be released in the *Star Wars* series, this epic battle between evil empire required a score of epic proportions. John Williams supplied marking 117 of the film's 127 minutes' running time for musical accompa-little of his score uses synthesisers or ethnic instruments – he preferred instead to use the symphony orchestra for its quality of delivery. The successful theme from the previous movie *Star Wars* (1977), with its heroic brass fanfares and off-beat chordal accompaniment, is reused in the opening. It is also reprised during battle sequences as a leitmotif for the rebels.

An important new march theme is composed for Darth Vader, who assumes a greater narrative importance in this film. It is derived from a major triad but accompanied by minor chords. The resultant clashes underline his evil nature, although the tonal confusion could also be interpreted as representing the two conflicting sides of his character:

**Williams, 'Darth Vader's Imperial March' from *The Empire Strikes Back***

The first time we hear this theme is when we view Darth Vader's battle fleet, his actual appearance being slightly later and filmed from behind. The theme appears on numerous occasions, always associated with Darth Vader and often as a straight statement on brass.

During the extended underscoring of the escape from the city, all the leitmotifs undergo various developments – changing into the minor, undergoing augmentation or diminution, and appearing in combination – to reflect the twists and turns in the character's fortunes.

Although there is a considerable amount of action music in the film, there are passages of a more relaxed nature, such as the eerie, impressionistic music for the planet Dagobar – scored for high chromatic strings, woodwind solos and harp – or the expansive love theme that gradually develops and is used as a grandiose out-take.

# James Horner (b.1953)

This young American (but British-trained) composer has the ability, much like Jerry Goldsmith, to write music for a wide range of films, from sci-fi (*Star Trek – the Wrath of Khan*, 1982; *Cocoon*, 1985) to those aimed at children (*Casper*, 1995), action films (*Legends of the Fall*, 1994; *Braveheart*, 1995) and blockbusters (*Titanic*, 1997). He has a gift for lyrical melody and often presents his main themes in a chorale-like scoring. However, he is very capable of enhancing exciting action sequences. The music for *Aliens* (1986), for example,

For an example of Horner's use of chorale-like scoring, see the launch sequence in *Apollo 13* (1995) or the main titles from *Courage Under Fire* (1996).

combines electronics and harmonic tone clusters with a large percussion battery and a full-size orchestra.

### Titanic (1997)

This big-budget movie has a soundtrack that has made more money for the studio than any other film to date, remaining at the top of the American album charts for 16 weeks. Horner composed it with the Irish singer Enya's style of music in mind (she had originally been approached to produce the music but declined). There is a significant Irish folk influence in much of the melodic material, such as the cue 'Unable to Stay, Unable to Leave'. The abandon of the ceilidh music contrasts neatly with the diegetic string music in the ship's lounge. Passages from actual folk tunes can also be heard, such as 'The Leaving of Liverpool'.

One particular cue worth examining is when the ship is being launched ('Take Her to Sea, Mr Murdoch'). The underscore for this cue features rolling lower strings for the movement of the hull, a quasi-diegetic ship's bell, a synthesised choir and a sweeping string melody as the ship moves out into the deeper water. The music and the action follow the stage convention of compressed time for the sake of the narrative, as such a departure in real time would take much longer.

The film's signature song – 'My Heart Will Go On', sung by Celine Dion – lifted music sales to an incredibly high degree and contributed significantly towards the overall success of the film.

# Howard Shore (b.1946)

Shore is a Canadian-born composer, trained at the Berklee College of Music, who has worked with a number of prestigious directors. He has collaborated with the independent film-maker David Cronenberg, who explores the relationship between the body and the mind through horror and sci-fi films. Shore's scores for *The Fly* (1986) and *eXistenZ* (1999) complement the unsettling subject matter well, combining progressive orchestral sounds with electronic effects. He also uses jazz: his score for Tim Burton's *Ed Wood* (1994) combines jazz and Cuban music with spooky theremin lines and the music he produced for *Naked Lunch* (1991) uses recordings of jazz licks by Charlie Parker, combined with Ornette Coleman's sax improvisations, against a scored orchestral background.

More recently he has moved towards scoring more mainstream productions, including *The Silence of the Lambs* (1991) and *The Game* (1997). His most successful work commercially has been for the *Lord of the Rings* series (2001, 2002, 2003).

### The Lord of the Rings: The Fellowship of the Ring (2001)

The trilogy of films of Tolkien's *Lord of the Rings* was the biggest film production at the start of the 21st century. Shore produced an expansive orchestral score to match the epic proportions of the storyline, which deals with the triumph of good over evil, achieved by the combined efforts of a team of hobbits, elves, dwarves, men, a wizard, and other imagined creatures.

His score, like some of those by James Horner, is heavily influenced by Irish music, just as Tolkien's fictional world is influenced by Celtic mythology. The cue 'Many Meetings' is based on a simple string and then clarinet melody, reflecting the domesticity of the scene:

**Shore, 'Many Meetings' from *Lord of the Rings: The Fellowship of the Ring***

Shore darkens this for the slightly later cue, 'The Ring Goes South', by transferring it to horns, transposing it into A major and removing its simple harmonic accompaniment, stating it against a tremolando dominant pedal.

Whereas *Titanic* failed to enlist Enya, in *this* film her voice is used for 'The Council of Elrond' and 'May it Be' – songs she composed and performed herself.

Shore employs Wagnerian sonorities, Romantic, extended string themes, and scary choral chanting used as a leitmotif for the nine ringwraiths and for action cues such as 'The Black Rider' and 'The Bridge of Khazad Dum'. Quasi-religious choral music is employed for 'Lothlorien' and 'The Great River', suggesting the pantheistic message. However, considering Shore's adventurous musical career, he composed a relatively traditional score for the large undertaking of this massive trilogy. This was probably shrewd as album sales have mirrored the resounding commercial success of the film.

The Argonath – statues of the Kings of Old – are approached from the river by the travellers.
Rising voices lead to grandiose strings and brass enhancing the majesty of the huge edifices.

# 15. WORLD CINEMA

It is a challenging task to try to summarise the whole of world cinema in a few paragraphs. Over the history of filmmaking a number of countries have consistently produced high quality work and to enable foreign language films to be represented a few composers that have written notable soundtracks have been selected.

## European cinema

As the continent of Europe includes many varied languages and cultures so this diversity is reflected in the types of films that are produced. Expressionist, New Wave and other forms of art cinema and issue-based social drama are to be found working independently of the global influence of Hollywood. A similar diversity can be found in the music written for such films. France and Italy are chosen to represent European cinema examining two films that have a more popular appeal, whilst the contribution made by Spain, Germany, Eastern Europe and Scandinavia is acknowledged.

## Yann Tiersen (b. 1970)

French cinema is known for its subtlety. It favours slow-to-emerge plots and strong characterisation, human relationships and tension and is less comfortable with grandiose gestures.

Yann Tiersen reflects these tendencies perfectly. He prefers to work with small acoustic ensembles with unusual instrumental combinations. Born in Brittany in 1970 he was classically trained and he developed a musical style that owed much to the tongue-in-cheek language of Erik Satie whilst incorporating some techniques from the minimalist composers. His love of unusual acoustic instruments is illustrated by his third music album Le Phare (1998), on which he played a huge variety of instruments, including violins, accordion, piano, mandolins, guitar, typewriter, saucepans, tam-tam, banjo, harpsichord, oud, acoustic guitars, toy piano, vibraphone, cello, melodica, chimes, bicycles and bontempi organ. Some tracks were used for the soundtrack of the award winning film *Amélie*.

### Amélie (*Le Fabuleux Destin d'Amélie Poulain*) (2001)

This story of a young, lonely Parisian girl finding love is set around a café in Montmartre where she is a waitress. Amélie (Audrey Tautou) is interested in the small details of human behaviour, and when she finds an old tin box with a young boy's precious possessions hidden away behind the wall in her flat she sets off to trace the original owner. Later she picks up a photo album made from discarded photo-booth pictures and falls in love with its creator.

Tiersen uses three main groups of instruments sometimes in combination:

- **Piano**: The music is used mostly for reflective moments. Slow melodies in octaves with rippling accompaniments reminiscent of Chopin are used when the focus is on Amélie's personal concerns – in her flat, the return of her goldfish to the wild, a list of those things she gets pleasure from etc

- **Accordion:** This is featured whenever there is hurrying around, particularly in the streets, or when Amélie is busy. Light waltz music is used, sometimes made busier with flowing quaver accompaniment. In addition solo melodic notes are used for tense moments such as when the old tin box is opened in a phone box or when Amélie is setting up the greengrocer's flat with practical jokes.

- **Tuned percussion**: frequently used to double a melody line. One telling moment is when the tin box is first opened and tinkling glockenspiels create a sense of magic. Later this develops with the addition of pizzicato and arco strings.

Amélie (Audrey Tautou) discovers the hidden tin box

There are several identifiable themes, but the most memorable appears first when she begins to fall in love; this reaches its full flow when she is united with the young artist at the end of the film. Although it is still an accordion playing this most of the other instruments join in to strengthen its delivery.

Music is rarely used during dialogue but contributes hugely to the atmosphere of the film, setting different scenes and moods and enhancing the role of the narrator. In contrast to the acoustic music, electronic effects are used for moments of drama.

# Nicola Piovani (b. 1946)

This composer works in a largely light-classical style. He has produced music for the veteran Italian director Federico Fellini and has over 130 film scores to his credit, also working in musical theatre and chamber music genres. In 1998 he won an Oscar for the score of the war-time film *La Vita è bella*.

### La Vita è bella (1997)

This film can be divided into two distinct halves. It begins with a wonderfully sunny Mediterranean-Italian melody played on woodwinds and trumpet with a beguine-like rhythmic accompaniment complete with mandolins. This theme permeates the whole of the first half and comes to represent life, family and happiness. It fits with the likeable comic nature of the main character Guido (Roberto Benigni). A second slow, more reflective theme is associated with romantic love.

Halfway through the mood changes entirely as Guido, his wife, and their charming little boy are transported to a Jewish concentration camp by the Nazis. The music lacks direct melody here and instead a series of dark minor chords on sustained strings create a mood of foreboding. Guido attempts to remain cheerful and there is a reference to the main theme when some German children visit the camp. A march version of the main tune, complete with a brassy tuba bass line is used when the prisoners leave the camp accompanied by their American rescuers.

Piovani has produced perfect music for the difficult tragicomic subject matter.

# India

Indian films have had a huge influence right across southern Asia and the Middle East. The Bollywood industry based in Mumbai produces large numbers of films in the Hindi language that have become popular worldwide. They are renowned for their big-budget productions, with a formulaic content that includes song and dance and emotionally-charged melodrama. Running parallel to this commercial approach was a more realistic film school based in Bengal with film-makers such as Satyajit Ray.

# A. R. Rahman (b. 1966)

Rahman is a massively influential composer and performer who has produced so much music that he is now rated as one of the world's top selling recording artists. His early musical experiences were as a keyboardist in bands in India but later graduated in Western classical music from Trinity College of Music in London.

After working on soundtracks for adverts his first feature scores were for films in the Tamil language, winning an award for his very first venture, *Roja* (1992). Later he worked with films in the Hindi tradition and most recently won an Oscar for the soundtrack of the British-produced *Slumdog Millionaire* (2008). His style is difficult to categorise because of its many influences: Carnatic (a branch of Indian classical music, he frequently uses for his vocals), Hindustani, Qawwali (an ancient Persian Muslim genre) Western classical, and even the street dance styles of Indian pop music.

### Guru (2007)

This is the story of a poor boy made good. His name is Gurukant (Abishek Bachchan) and he travels to Turkey to seek his fortune in the textile industry. The romantic element is supplied by his love for his wife Sujata (Aishwarya Rai) – initially a marriage of convenience.

In the grand tradition of Bollywood there are the various set song and dance routines for which Rahman writes memorable music. These vary in their musical styles from Turkish ('Mayya Mayya' features female vocals and arab flute) to folk-influenced (male vocals with acoustic sounds of tablas and plucked strings) and love-ballads ('Tere Bina' with male vocals, female semi-chorus and orchestral string backing).

### Rahman, the love ballad 'Tere Bina' from *Guru*

However, Rahmen is much more than just a song writer. He creates underscore that is extremely effective. One telling moment in the film is when Guru and Sujata are remembering how their relationship developed after a difficult meeting with his company. There are flashbacks of various moments and the tune above – 'Tere Bina' – played. Guru then crashes to the floor with a stroke and the music is transformed with electronically processed strings pulling on our emotions and the remnants of the old love theme attempting in vain to cut through the texture.

The film won Rahman awards for music direction and best background score.

# The Far East

Japan has a long history of film-making which included the legendary director Akira Kurosawa (*Seven Samurai*, 1954) and Korea is well-known for the films of Park Chan-Wook. Mainland China has only emerged as a major force in more recent times as changes in the political situation have allowed more artistic freedom. It has produced international hits with *Farewell my Concubine* (1993), *Crouching Tiger, Hidden Dragon* (2000) and *Hero* (2002).

# Tan Dun (b.1957)

Tan Dun was born and brought up in a Chinese village but got his first big break touring with Beijing opera. He studied with the Japanese composer Toru Takemitsu (1930–1996), himself both a concert composer and writer of film scores and he was much influenced by American avant-garde composers, particularly the minimalists. The cellist Yo-Yo Ma was featured in Tan Dun's commission Symphony 1997, written for the handing over of Hong Kong to mainland China, and he played again for the composer's award winning film soundtrack in 2000. His music has been used for the Beijing 2008 Olympics and the internet search engine Google commissioned his Internet Symphony No.1 'Eroica' in the same year.

### Crouching Tiger, Hidden Dragon (2000)

The composer utilises a combination of Western orchestral forces with Chinese traditional instruments to create a score of haunting beauty. The story is a historical Chinese costume drama that combines fight sequences with a love story. For the former, Dun employs dramatic percussion forces, the drums complementing the energetic action. The love element is covered by a sweeping string theme, and binding the score together are the haunting cello solos of Yo-Yo Ma. Orchestral strings frequently work in combination with Chinese traditional instruments (such as the two string erhu) creating long atmospheric passages that do not attempt to mirror the visuals.

Despite the film's awards for its soundtrack, much of the music is performable as a concert piece away from the cinema.

# 16. COMPILATION SOUNDTRACKS

Before concluding this overview of film music, the subject of music imported into films from external sources, serving to supply the full soundtrack, should be mentioned. One famous example is Stanley Kubrick's *2001: A Space Odyssey* (1968). For this film, Kubrick decided to use the temp track for the music, rejecting the score composed by Alex North. He felt that the music of Richard and Johann Strauss and György Ligeti among others, included on the temp track, would provide the right atmosphere.

Kubrick followed this film with the controversial *Clockwork Orange* (1971), which also uses imported classical music, although this time its use is specified in part by the plot. Here, a sense of irony is achieved through the use of Beethoven's optimistic Symphony No 9 (1824) and Rossini's colourful overtures to *William Tell* (1829) and *The Thieving Magpie* (1817) to accompany scenes of extreme violence.

> On occasions in *Clockwork Orange*, the music is arranged for analogue synthesisers by Wendy Carlos, adding to the surreal atmosphere.

There have been a considerable number of films, particularly over the last few decades, in which directors have preferred not to use a composer to write an underscore. A common alternative approach is to import a series of popular music singles tracks, to enhance the overall mood of the story, add style or simply to increase the revenue. A few famous films which have adopted this approach are set out below, alongside some of the bands that contributed to the soundtracks:

- *The Graduate* (1967) – haunting music by Simon and Garfunkel to complement the film's portrayal of the confusion of growing up
- *Easy Rider* (1969) – a rock soundtrack to match the counter-culture youth message by Steppenwolf, Jimi Hendrix and Bob Dylan
- *American Graffiti* (1973) – nostalgic use of rock and roll from Chuck Berry and Bill Hayley
- *Saturday Night Fever* (1977) – disco from the Bee Gees
- *Trainspotting* (1996) – music to set the scene of drug addicts living in Edinburgh, provided by Iggy Pop, Lou Reed, Primal Scream and Underworld.

## Pulp Fiction (1994)

This story of American gangster violence was directed by Quentin Tarantino as an independent production; it was awarded the prestigious Palme d'Or at the Cannes Film Festival. The film has been classified by many film critics as post-modern, not only because its storyline is non-linear (time does not move forward logically) but also because of its cultural influences, including the importance of music tracks, existing as separate entities within the film. The tracks are taken from a 1950s pop repertoire. They are often chosen by the characters in the film themselves, and therefore have a diegetic impact; however they also frequently make oblique comments on the action.

The soundtrack is instrumental in establishing the mood of the film, either by enhancing it (for example, in the scene in Jack Rabbit Slim's club) or serving as an ironic contrast to the violence shown on screen. Interesting examples of these techniques are listed below:

- Following a period of no music in the opening scene – an attempted robbery in a restaurant – a title soundtrack suddenly bursts forth, featuring the exciting sound of a lead Fender Stratocaster guitar playing in an upbeat surf-rock instrumental ('Misirlou', performed by Dick Dale and His Del-Tones). This sets the high level of energy in the film, which is sustained by additional surf-rock instrumental tracks as it progresses. As Vincent Vega (John Travolta) drives to Mia's (Uma Thurman's) apartment, after taking drugs, his hazy yet excited mood is enhanced by a guitar track that uses reverb and a tremolo arm, creating a wobbly effect.

- When Vincent enters Mia's apartment, we are unsure whether the music (Dusty Springfield singing 'Son of a Preacher Man') is diegetic or not. At first we believe it to be background as there is a clear visual of a static tape recorder in the room. However, we discover that Mia is controlling the music from another room. First, we detect a change in volume level when the camera cuts to her room, and then we see a close up of the record arm being lifted. Later, Mia takes another step in controlling the situation when she presses the tape recorder's start button to play a track entitled 'Girl, You'll Be a Woman Soon' (by Neil Diamond, performed by Urge Overkill). The track's lyrics also serve to provide comment on the action.

- Mia's drug overdose is the climax of a series of music tracks after which there is no music for a further 30 minutes. This is a good example of Tarantino using music to control the pace of the film, a technique which is more usually found in composed film scores rather than compilation soundtracks.

A useful resource on the music used in Tarantino's films can be found in *Film Music: critical approaches* by Kevin Donnelly (chapter 10, Edinburgh University Press, 2001).

# 17. EXAMINATIONS

This book, in addition to giving background information on the film industry, is mostly concerned with composers and how they use their skills to write music that will enhance the viewer's enjoyment and the overall effectiveness of films. In the examination system for England and Wales students and teachers are given a great deal of choice when it comes to how they approach the study of film:

■ **WJEC A level Film Studies** expects analysis of a film extract concentrating on one of five 'micro-features', which includes sound, and a creative project needs to be undertaken which could well involve information on, or employment of, a sound-track. Reflective analysis of films such as *Vertigo* (1958) with its stunning score written by Bernard Herrmann will clearly need some understanding of composing techniques.

■ The **Edexcel BTEC Nationals** provides some very relevant units:
  ■ BTEC music: unit 20 – music and sound for the moving image
  ■ BTEC creative media production: unit 38 – soundtrack production for the moving image
  ■ Units in composition and film studies are also available.

■ This book will also be valuable for general written work for the **Creative and Media Diploma**. In addition, the techniques used by composers could be adopted by students in their practical projects. The following extract from the Diploma specification is a case in point:

> **Project**: You can do your project about anything you like because you choose the topic, and how you're going to present your work. You'll need to show all the things you've learnt on your Diploma course, but what you do it on is up to you. It could be a written piece of work, like a report; an investigation or something practical, for example putting on a production at your school or college, doing the lighting and sound as well as the show, or creating a short film.
> Sourced from: *http://yp.direct.gov.uk/diplomas/subjects/Creative_Media/the_course/*

■ **AS/A Level**: students of **Music** and **Music Technology** are often expected to compose music for the moving image. Some analytical skills are also expected. OCR unit G355 (composing 2) offers film and television as an option. AQA A2 music also includes a unit on music for film and theatre (Unit 4). The following is an extract from the Edexcel music specification:

> **Area of study – applied music**
> **Topic 3: music for film and television**
> Students should consider how music can be used to take the listener on a complex and musically satisfying emotional journey in parallel with the moving image on film and television (and therefore often independently of traditional music forms and structures).

- The composition brief for **Edexcel A level Music Technology** includes music for film and television. It is difficult for teachers to tackle the sometimes dry academic aspects of composing but if students are fortunate enough to be able to choose a topic based on the moving image then teachers will be able to refer to the many and varied techniques used by film composers and even illustrate them with a film screening in class.

- Finally the **musicianship courses** offered by the conservatoires must not be forgotten. For example the **AMusTCL** from Trinity College of Music has a section where students have to answer in-depth questions on film scores, many of which are featured in *Film Music in Focus*.

# 18. EPILOGUE AND RESOURCES

Having watched the films described in this book and studied the analyses, you should be more aware of the contribution that music can make to the overall cinematic experience. From the earliest days of silent movies to the digital surround sound of the modern movie theatre, music has consistently been acknowledged by film-makers as an essential contribution to a film's ability to communicate its message or entertain a critical public. However, modern technologies are set to turn the world of commercial media upside down.

At the time of writing, digital software programmes are empowering everyone interested in the arts to take part in the creative aspects of film and music production, and the internet is facilitating the distribution of the end products. Sites such as MySpace (www.myspace.com) host music from young indie bands, and even supergroups such as Radiohead distribute their work without recourse to major record labels. Amateur film-makers share their work on YouTube (www.youtube.com) and there are films readily downloadable from a number of internet providers. This democratisation of the media can only be for the good, with people feeding off each other's ideas, distilling into a melting pot that combines variety with accessibility.

One of the roles of education, then, is to encourage the study of the great films of the past to inform the cutting-edge developments of the future. The following resources are recommended for students who want to study film music in greater depth, whether for creative or academic purposes.

# Resources

### Books

Royal S Brown, *Overtones and Undertones: reading film music* (University of California Press 1994) – a perceptive, in-depth look at the relationship between sight and sound – scholarly yet readable.

William Darby and Jack Du Bois, *American Film Music: major composers, techniques, trends 1915–1990* (McFarland Press 1990) – a comprehensive book on Hollywood film, with lots of music examples and analysis.

Richard Davis, *Complete Guide to Film Scoring* (Berklee Press 2000) – this explains the technical process very well, also including some interviews with composers.

Kathryn Kalinak, *Settling the Score* (The University of Winconsin Press 1993) – readable, thoughtful and non-technical with analysis of several different styles.

Fred Karlin, *Listening to Movies* (Schirmer 1994) – a comprehensive book on Hollywood movies, packed with information.

Roy M Prendergast, *Film Music – A Neglected Art* (W W Norton and Company, 2nd edition, 1992) – a good history of film music, with musical examples and some technical information.

Mark Russell and James Young, *Film Music (Screencraft series)* (Focal Press 2000) – a beautifully produced book with full colour pictures, composer interviews and an excellent music CD.

Paul Terry, *Musicals in Focus* (Rhinegold Education, 2nd edition, 2009) – an introductory guide to musicals.

Tony Thomas, *Music for the Movies* (Silman-James Press, 2nd edition, 1997) – a history of film music with a focus on individual composers.

## Websites

**www.imdb.com** – database of information on all films past and present.

**www.filmsite.org** – lots of analysis of films, including substantial plot summaries.

**www.mfiles.co.uk** – music files and lots of information on music for film.

**http://filmsound.org** – excellent site for technical info.

**www.filmtracks.com** – modern soundtrack reviews.

**www.bfi.org.uk** – British Film Institute website.

**www.mediaknowall.com** – a good starting point for media studies students.

**www.moviegrooves.com** – free audio samples of film tracks.

# GLOSSARY

**A cappella**. Unaccompanied singing (usually choral).

**Added sixth**. A chord of root, third and fifth with an added sixth making four notes in total. Mildly discordant.

**Arco**. Played with a bow.

**Atonal**. Music that avoids a sense of key, often discordant.

**Augmentation**. Notes are increased in length by an equal amount in a musical passage, creating broadening. *See* **diminution**.

**Basso profondo**. A male voice of exceedingly low range.

**Bitonal**. Music that uses two keys simultaneously.

**Cantabile**. In a smooth singing style.

**Chorale**. Hymn-like.

**Chromatic**. Music that uses a large number of notes outside the key.

**Counterpoint**. In music, counterpoint is concerned with the interplay of independent melodic lines. In film studies, the word is often applied to music that is opposite to the expected sound implied by the visuals (as opposed to 'parallel', which is used to describe music that complements the visuals).

**Cue**. A section of music that is timed to fit a specific portion of visuals.

**Diatonic**. Music that has notes mostly within the key. Opposite of **chromatic**.

**Diegetic music**. Music that appears to originate from something on screen (also known as 'source music' or 'in-vision music'). This might include source music from the set such as a car radio or a band in a nightclub, or sound effects such as guns in the distance or screeching car brakes. *See* **non-diegetic.**

**Dissonant**. Harsh and discordant.

**Diminished seventh**. Four note chord made from intervals of a minor third e.g. C# dim 7th is: C#, E, G, B♭.

**Diminution**. Notes are shortened in length by an equal amount in a musical passage, creating excitement. *See* **augmentation.**

**Dominant**. The fifth note of the scale.

**Film noir**. A term used to describe Hollywood crime productions, particularly those that focus upon moral ambiguity and sexual motivation. The classic film noir period is usually regarded as spanning the early 1940s to the late 1950s.

**Flutter-tonguing**. A technique, most commonly used on the flute (though it can also be employed on the clarinet and some brass instruments), which involves the trilling of the letter 'R' while playing to produce rapid note repetition.

**Fugato**. A section of music which uses fugal style, though not necessarily following strict fugal procedure entirely.

**Functional music**. Harmonic progressions that follow their expected course.

**Hit point**. An exact point during a cue when music or sound effects match a moment on screen.

**Leitmotif**. (from German, leitmotiv). A term first applied to the music of Wagner, it refers to a frequently recurring musical motif or theme that represents a specific person, thing or abstract idea.

**Lombardic**. A reverse dotted rhythm (for example a semiquaver followed by a dotted quaver).

**Lower partials**. The resonances of the harmonic series that are closest to the fundamental note.

**Melisma**. A device whereby two or more notes are sung during one syllable of text.

**Mickey-mousing**. A technique frequently used in cartoons where the music attempts to represent every little physical movement on screen.

**MIDI**. Musical Instrumental Digital Interface. A standard tool for connecting and remotely operating electronic instruments and related devices such as computers and effects units.

**MIDI file**. Digital data file containing MIDI information; functions in most software.

**Motif (or motive)**. A short thematic strand of only a few notes.

**Motto theme**. Similar to 'leitmotif' – a theme which recurs (and is sometimes transformed) throughout a work.

**Modal**. Music that uses modes instead of scales. These avoid the use of sharps or flats and use just the 'white' notes of the keyboard. Each one has its own character. The common ones used in film music are Dorian, Phrygian, Mixolydian and Aeolian – beginning on D, E, G, and A respectively.

**Motivic development**. Music that uses a range of techniques (e.g. repetition or inversion) to develop a small motive and move forward.

**Non-diegetic music**. Music which has been composed to accompany events on screen but which visibly is not part of the action (for instance, music to accompany a car chase or to highlight the emotions of a conversation between two characters). Also referred to as 'underscore' or 'incidental' music. *See* **diegetic**.

**Ostinato**. Repeated pattern of notes above or below which music can change.

**Out-take**. A section of a film or music recording which is removed during the editing process.

**Opera buffa**. 'Comic opera' in Italian, the opposite of opera seria. A style in which comedy is derived from everyday characters. Notable composers who worked within this style include Mozart, Rossini and Donizetti.

**Partials**. The resonances of the harmonic series and the constituent parts of a sound. Removal of some of them can change the tone quality.

**Pedal (or pedal point)**. A sustained or repeated note against which changing harmonies are heard. A pedal on the dominant creates excitement and the feeling that the tension must be resolved by moving to the tonic. A pedal on the tonic anchors the music to its key note. A pedal can be created, for example, on both tonic and dominant – a double pedal. If a pedal occurs in an upper part, rather than the bass, it is called an inverted pedal.

**Pentatonic**. A five note scale often found in folk music. Two common versions: major – C, D, E, G, A and minor – C, E♭, F, G, B♭

**Phrygian**. A mode, often associated with Spanish or Arabic music, that uses the interval sequence of the white notes on the keyboard from E to E.

**Polyphonic**. As used most frequently today, this term describes the texture made up of two or more melodies sounding together.

**Post-Romantic**. A style of music written mostly between 1890 and 1910 which featured a expansive sound. Composers include Mahler, Elgar and Sibelius. Much favoured by Hollywood film composers.

**Programme music**. Concert hall music that follows a story line or illustrates a picture, e.g. Mendelssohn's Hebrides Overture.

**Retrograde**. Backwards.

**Recitative**. Style of singing found in opera where the vocal line copies the inflexions and rhythms of speech.

**Ritornello**. A passage of music (most often associated with Baroque arias and concertos) that keeps returning.

**Screenplay**. Script written especially for film or television.

**Sequence**. In melody this is where a pattern of notes is repeated higher or lower. Often used for building or easing tension.

**Short score**. Simplified orchestral score where instruments share staves e.g. woodwind, brass strings and bass are reduced to four staves in total.

**Stop motion**. An animation technique that involves taking a photo, then advancing the subject of the photo a small amount, then taking another photo, then repeating the process. The photos are then run in sequence to produce animated movement.

**Source music**. *See* **diegetic**.

**Suspension**. Where one part of the music is held back while the other moves on. It is usual for the suspended part to catch up and this is called its resolution.

**Synchronisation**. The process of marrying up music and film. Usually handled within a sequencer, sometimes communicating externally with a video recorder using timecode (SMPTE).

**Syncopation**. Unexpected rhythmic accent.

**Temp track**. Temporary music brought in part-way through the filming process to stand in place of music still to be composed. It is used to give the producer and studio executives a better idea of how the film will turn out than if there were no music at all. One famous example is the use of 'Mars' from Holst's 'The Planets' suite for the Imperial Stormtroopers in *Star Wars*.

**Tonal, tonality**. Major and minor keys.

**Tone clusters**. Small groups of adjacent notes played simultaneously creating a percussive or crunchy effect.

**Tone rows**. 12 note scales devised by composers of the serial tradition. They were an order of all the notes of the chromatic scale and used to produce music often of an atonal nature. In films, composers used them for scary or frightening moments.

**Tremolo strings**. Rapid movements of the bow on a single note resulting in a dramatic and energetic sound.

**Triad**. The standard three note chord of root, third and fifth.

**Tritone**. An interval of an augmented 4th or diminished 5th traditionally associated with evil and menace. e.g. C to F♯.

**Tutti**. Everyone together i.e. an orchestral tutti is the whole orchestra.

**Underscore**. *See* **non-diegetic music**.

**Walking quavers**. Constantly moving quavers creating the sense of walking along. e.g. common walking bass in swing jazz.

# INDEX

# Index

## Picture credits

Cover image – Kobal/Waner Bros

p. 5 – Getty Images
p. 7 – Getty Images
p. 12 – Getty Images
p. 17 – Getty Images
p. 20 – Kobal/RKO
p. 21 – Lebrecht Music & Arts
p. 22 – Kobal/Warner Bros
p. 24 – Lebrecht Music & Arts
p. 25 – Kobal/Selznick/United Artists
p. 28 – Kobal/Paramount
p. 31 – Kobal/United Artists
p. 32 – Kobal/Columbia
p. 34 – Kobal/P.E.A
p. 36 – Getty Images
p. 38 – Kobal/Paramount
p. 40 – Kobal/Paramount
p. 42 – Kobal/Paramount
p. 43 – Kobal/Castle Rock Entertainment/Michael Weinstein
p. 45 – Kobal/RKO
p. 46 – Kobal/United Artists
p. 49 – Kobal/Columbia
p. 51 – Kobal/Focus Features/Studio Canal/Guy Ferrandis
p. 53 – BFI Stills
p. 57 – Kobal/Touchstone/Burton/Di Novi
p. 59 – Kobal/20th Century Fox
p. 63 – Kobal/Ladd Company/Warner Bros
p. 69 – Kobal/Dreamworks/Universal/Jaap Buitendijk
p. 71 – Kobal/Focus Features/Alex Bailey
p. 74 – Kobal/Galatee Films/France 2
p. 76 – Kobal/BFI/United Artists
p. 77 – Kobal/Institute for Regional Education
p. 79 – Kobal/LucasFilm/20th Century Fox
p. 83 – Kobal/New Line/Saul Zaentz/Wing Nut
p. 85 – Kobal/UGC/Studio Canal

# Copyright acknowledgements

All metronome markings included in the music examples in this book have been provided by the author. They are indications based on recordings of the music in question, and do not necessarily reflect the original scores exactly.